THE HISTORY (

With memories of Sunday afternoon tea
with my parents and sister.

THE HISTORY OF TEA

by

CLAIRE HOPLEY

REMEMBER WHEN

First published in Great Britain in 2009 by
Remember When
an imprint of
Pen & Sword Books Ltd
47 Church Street
Barnsley
South Yorkshire
S70 2AS

ISBN 978-1-84468-030-6

A CIP catalogue record for this book is available from the British Library.

Typeset in 12/14 Palatino by
Concept, Huddersfield, West Yorkshire

Printed and bound in England
by CPI UK

Pen & Sword Books Ltd incorporates the imprints of Pen & Sword Aviation, Pen & Sword Maritime, Pen & Sword Military, Wharncliffe Local History, Pen & Sword Select, Pen & Sword Military Classics, Leo Cooper, Remember When, Seaforth Publishing and Frontline Publishing.

For a complete list of Pen & Sword titles please contact
PEN & SWORD BOOKS LIMITED
47 Church Street, Barnsley, South Yorkshire, S70 2AS, England
E-mail: enquiries@pen-and-sword.co.uk
Website: www.pen-and-sword.co.uk

Contents

Introduction

In the Eighteenth Century Dr. Samuel Johnson confessed himself 'a hardened and shameless tea drinker', ruefully admitting that his kettle had 'scarcely time to cool' because he drank tea from morning until midnight. Millions of us share his enthusiasm for tea, needing it at breakfast, with mid-morning breaks, and as a restorative at the end of the day. Though afternoon tea as a daily event is no longer a daily event for most of us, it's more than ever delightful as a special-occasion treat, its very rarity encouraging serious splurging on tiered dishes of enticing little sandwiches and pretty pastries, on strawberries or scones – or both – with lots of cream.

Yet for much of our history tea was unknown. It arrived in the 1650s, quickly became wildly fashionable, and within a few decades tea had become the daily beverage of most people.

Why did they choose tea rather than coffee, which arrived in Britain at about the same time as tea? Where did they buy it? How did they make and drink it? How did tea-times such as afternoon tea and high tea come about? Most importantly, who drank tea together and what was its social significance?

To answer these questions this book traces the history of tea through many sources, but most importantly, it focuses on novels, plays, poems and other literary texts to explore the social and emotional aspects of tea-drinking. From Samuel Pepys, who drank tea as a protection against illness, to George Orwell, who explained how to get the best out of the meagre wartime ration; from Congreve's Millamant, who insisted on being 'sole empress of my tea-table' to Jane Austen's Fanny Price, Charlotte Brontë's Jane Eyre, and even J.K. Rowling's Hagrid, writers and their characters have joined Dr. Johnson in loving and relying on tea. However, what it has meant to them has varied over the centuries. Understanding literary tea-times illuminates the role tea has played in British life. It also often sheds new light on scenes such as Jane Eyre's tea with her headmistress, the hotel tea Pip tries to buy for Estella in *Great Expectations*, and the tea Lily Bart pours for the men she thinks about marrying in Edith Wharton's *The House of Mirth.*

Claire Hopley

Acknowledgements

I WISH to acknowledge the generosity of the many authors, their agents and publishers who have given permission to quote from their works. Quotations from *Murphy* by Samuel Beckett are used with permission of Faber and Faber, Limited. Lines from Sir John Betjeman's poem *In a Bath Tea Shop* from *Collected Poems* © 1970 are reproduced by generous permission of John Murray (Publishers). A.P. Watt gave permission on behalf of the Executors of the Estate of K.S.P. McDowell to quote from the Mapp and Lucia novels of E.F. Benson. Quotations from *The Last September* and *The Heat of the Day* by Elizabeth Bowen are copyright © Elizabeth Bowen 1929, 1949, and reproduced with the kind permission of Curtis, Brown Group Ltd., London on behalf of the estate of Elizabeth Bowen. Rodgers, Coleridge and White Ltd. gave permission to quote from Anita Desai's novel *Fasting, Feasting* (1999). Arthur Dobrin kindly gave permission to quote his poem *The Wine of the Poor*. Permission to quote from Graham Greene's *Travels with my Aunt* (1969) comes from David Higham Associates, who also gave generous permission to quote from Molly Keane's *Good Behaviour* (1981) and *Taking Chances* (1929). A.P. Watt gave permission on behalf of the Royal Literary Fund to quote from W. Somerset Maugham's *Of Human Bondage* (1915) and *Cakes and Ale* (1930). Sally Keefe Cohen, Literary Consultant to Hebb & Sheffer of Toronto, Canada kindly arranged for me to quote from *Anne of Green Gables* by L.M. Montgomery (1908). Extracts from *The Pie and the Patty Pan* by Beatrix Potter, copyright © Frederick Warne & Co., 1905 are reproduced with kind permission of Frederick Warne & Co. I thank Christopher Little Literary Agency for permission to quote from *Harry Potter and the Sorcerer's Stone* © J.K. Rowling, 1997. The quotations from May Sinclair's *The Cure of Souls* are reproduced by kind permission of Curtis Brown Group Ltd., London on behalf of the estate of May Sinclair copyright © 1925 May Sinclair. Quotations from Dylan Thomas's *Under Milk Wood: A Play for Voices* (1954) and *A Child's Christmas in Wales* (1955) are used with kind permission from David Higham Associates. I thank Elizabeth Swaffield of Wingham, New South Wales, for her generous permission to quote from *Lark Rise to Candleford* (1939) written by her grandmother, Flora Thompson. I thank Diana Rawston of Goodman Derrick LLP, a trustee of the estate of

P.L. Travers, for permission to quote from *Mary Poppins* (1934). I also thank HarperCollins Publishers Ltd. for permission to quote from *Little Grey Rabbit's Party* by © 1936 Alison Uttley. The Society of Authors generously gave permission for me to quote from Virginia Woolf's *Mrs. Dalloway* (1925) and *Between the Acts* (1941).

I want to thank Nancy Cahill and her sister Patricia for their kindness and generosity. I wish also to thank Nancy Gregg for reading a draft of Chapter 5. Katy Squires of Taylor's of Harrogate and John Harney of Harney and Sons, Millerton, New York arranged for me to see their production facilities and gave me information, for which I am very grateful. I want also to thank the Bramah Museum of Tea and Coffee, 40 Southwark Street, London SE1 for their help. Gwen Tudor helped me research museums and tea shops in Wales; Moira Brenard directed my attention to tea shops in Bristol; and George Ross of Edinburgh told me about tea in Scotland. I thank my sister Rona McAdam and in-laws Derek and Lillian Hopley, for driving and other help, and my husband Bob, for drinking tea, reading about tea clippers, and for listening to me natter on about tea.

CHAPTER 1

The Origins and Sources of Tea: China, Japan and India

Thank God for tea! What would the world do without tea? How did it exist? I am glad that I was not born before tea.

Reverend Sydney Smith

THE HISTORY of tea is jewelled with tales of adventure and commerce, stories of comfort in hardship and relief when things get better. At once the most domestic of beverages, tea is also the most elegant, the most evocative – and the most inspiring to writers.

Founding father

The story of the Chinese Emperor Shen Nung highlights the origin of tea. The founder of Chinese agriculture and skilled in medicine, Shen Nung drank nothing but boiled water. One day in 2737BC, he sat with his simmering water by a handsome tree. The breeze swayed through the leaves, wafting a few of them into his water. The fragrance was wonderful; the beverage deliciously stimulating. The tree, it turned out, was a tea tree, and in this way the first pot of tea serendipitously brewed itself. As the Emperor noted in his *Pen ts'ao* or *Medical Book,* tea does more than relieve ailments: 'It quenches thirst. It lessens the desire for sleep. It gladdens and cheers the heart.'

How true those observations are! Not so the tale of Shen Nung. Enchanting as it is, it cannot be literal fact. Tea leaves are dried and processed before being made into a pot of tea. More important, the earliest version of Shen Nung's book was not written until the Second or Third Century AD, and its references to tea date from that era, not from the dawn of Chinese history, when Shen Nung lived.

So the story about the Emperor and the tea leaves is a myth. But like all myths it explains why we do what we do, and it captures truths: tea uplifts the spirits and sharpens the mind; it soothes the sick and preserves the healthy; it charms; it entrances. Its discovery has been a blessing and a pleasure to the countless millions who have made it the world's most popular beverage.

Writers on tea

Writers have been some of the world's greatest tea lovers. From its earliest days, tea has inspired tales and poems. Soon after the beverage arrived in England in 1657, poet Edmund Waller highlighted its stimulating effect on poets' minds: 'Tea doth our fancy aid' he claimed. He called it 'the Muse's friend', noting its triumph over earlier inspirations:

Venus her Myrtle, Phoebus has his bays;
Tea both excels, . . .

Matthew Prior also linked tea to poets. In his 1687 poem *The City Mouse and the Country Mouse,* the Country Mouse confesses to Bundle that he had 'heard much talk of the Wits' Coffee House':

'Thither,' said Bundle, 'you shall go and see
Priests drinking coffee and Poets tea.'

A century later, Dr. Samuel Johnson confessed himself:

> *A hardened and shameless tea drinker, who has for many years diluted his meals with only the infusion of this fascinating plant; whose kettle has scarcely time to cool; who with tea amuses the evening, with tea solaces the midnight, and with tea welcomes the morning.*

Like Johnson, the romantic poet Percy Bysshe Shelley could put away countless cups of tea, and he loved tea-time foods. Thomas Hogg, his biographer noted:

> *Tea was ever grateful, cup after cup ... Like all persons of simple tastes, he retained his sweet tooth; he would greedily eat cakes, gingerbread and sugar; honey, preserved or stewed fruits with bread.*

In the 1940s, when gingerbread was rare and tea severely rationed, George Orwell devoted an *Evening Standard* article to how to make tea, detailing the eleven points necessary for 'wringing out of one's ration' twenty decent cups of tea a week.

Poets, tea and the pleasures of home

But tea does more than stimulate literary creativity; it also taps a golden lode of images. For poets, tea suggests home comforts. In England, William Cowper voiced these most memorably in his 1785 poem *The Task*:

> *Now stir the fire, and close the shutters fast*
> *Let fall the curtains, wheel the sofa round,*
> *And while the bubbling and loud-hissing urn*
> *Throws up a steamy column, and the cups*
> *That cheer but not inebriate, wait on each,*
> *So let us welcome peaceful evening in.*

For the Ninth-Century Chinese poet Po Chu-I cups of tea mark the routines of daily life:

After lunch – one short nap;
On waking up – two cups of tea.

If such routines are destroyed their memory becomes a hunger for past content. Rupert Brooke captured this in *The Old Vicarage, Grantchester*:

And does the clock still stand at ten to three,
And is there honey still for tea?

Conversely, the Twentieth-Century Japanese poet Shuntaro Tanikawa, looks ahead to memories to warm the future in his poem *Picnic to the Earth*:

Here I will keep on saying 'I have returned!'
As long as you repeat 'Welcome back!'
Here I will keep on returning again and again,
Here let's drink hot tea.
Here sitting together for a while
Let's have the refreshing wind touch us.

The tea-drinking characters of novelists and playwrights

Novelists and playwrights use tea-times to set a scene, convey character, develop relationships, and suggest feelings and ambience. When Algy eats the cucumber sandwiches he has ordered for Lady Bracknell at the beginning of Oscar Wilde's *The Importance of Being Earnest* the audience realises that he little fears the fire of this dragon aunt. All will clearly be well at the end of the play. Readers of Molly Keane's novels of Irish country-house life soon spot that anyone who is given an egg with their tea is being favoured – perhaps for sporting exploits, but also for personal charms. In contrast to the lavish Irish teas, the abstemious tea parties of the ladies of Mrs. Gaskell's *Cranford* exemplify the genteel economy of their lives. They cannot provide the eggs, the muffins, and the cakes that make tea-time a late-afternoon feast. Nonetheless, they reign over their tea-tables like the women in thousands of novels and plays, asserting a social position and controlling a domain.

In short, fictional tea-times tell us what it felt like to be taking tea in earlier centuries, capturing the pleasures that powered the economics of getting tea from tropical tea gardens and into British teacups, and vivifying tea-times of today by conjuring benign shades of tea-times past.

Origins and growth

Tea comes from the leaves of *Camellia sinensis*. Lovingly called 'the queen of camellias' by the Japanese tea historian Okakura Kakuzo, it is one of hundreds of important and beautiful plants that evolved in the botanical paradise of the Himalayas. These steep mountains stride the tropics, drawing monsoon-bearing winds up their heights. Tea thrives in heat and humidity, now not only in the Himalayas but in the mountains of Japan, Sri Lanka, Indonesia, Kenya and other places of similar climate.

Eating tea

Tea leaves were probably first eaten rather than drunk, maybe as long as 60,000 years ago. Early travellers reported that forest peoples in Thailand, Myanmar, and Assam chewed tea leaves. In the cold regions of Asia such as Tibet and Mongolia tea is still mixed with butter and meal to make a sustaining gruel rather than a drink. The Dong people of southern China make a festive soup of green tea leaves, mashed ginger and garlic served garnished with peanuts and puffed rice fried in teaseed oil.

Drinking tea

The legend of Shen Nung notwithstanding, the first unquestioned reference to drinking tea rather than chewing it, is in the *Erh Ya,* a Chinese annotated dictionary of 350AD, which explains that the leaves are brewed with boiling water, then drunk to improve eyesight, relieve lethargy, and dispel 'noxious gases of the body'. The boiling water needed to make tea certainly protected the residents of the populous Fifth-Century Chinese cities from the water-borne epidemics of cholera and typhoid that plagued large European towns until the end of the Nineteenth Century.

But tea has always been more than a herbal remedy. A Fifth-Century Chinese dictionary noted that it was a pleasant beverage that could lift the pall of a hangover. An emperor recorded in the Eighth-Century *Ch'a Ching* noted: 'The use of tea grows upon me surprisingly; I know not how it is but my fancy is awakened and my spirits exhilarated as if by wine.'

By this time drinking tea was so widespread that Ninth-Century Arab travellers reported that the Chinese government depended on the taxes on tea and salt for most of its revenue. Salt was actually used in tea, as were garlic, onions, orange peel, ginger and other spices.

Making tea Lu Yu's way

With tea well-established as both a popular drink and a polite amusement among connoisseurs, tea merchants prospered. In 780 they commissioned the poet Lu Yu to write a book about tea called *Ch'a Ching* – variously translated as *Tea Book, The Code of Tea* or *Classic of Tea.*

Lu Yu knew what he liked. Describing the characteristics of good tea leaves, he wrote that they should have:

> *Creases like the leather boots of Tartar horsemen, curl like the dewlap of the mighty bullock, unfold like the mist rising out of a ravine, gleam like a lake touched by a zephyr, and be wet and soft like fine earth newly swept by rain.*

Lu Yu despised all flavourings except salt, and advised using mountain spring water to make tea. Paraphrasing his words in limpid metaphors Okakura Kakuzo explained how to boil the water:

> *There are three stages of boiling: the first boil is when the little bubbles like the eye of fishes swim on the surface; the second boil is when the bubbles are like crystal beads rolling in a fountain; the third boil is when the billows surge wildly in the kettle. The cake tea is roasted before the fire until it becomes soft like a baby's arm and is shredded into powder between pieces of fine paper. Salt is put in the first boil, the tea in the second. At the third boil, a dipperful of cold water is put in the kettle to settle the tea and revive 'the youth of the water'. Then the beverage was poured into the cups and drunk. O nectar! The filmy leaflet hung like scaly clouds in a serene sky or floated like water lilies on emerald streams.*

Perhaps because of Lu Yu's encyclopaedic work, the Chinese abandoned onions, ginger and other strong flavourings, replacing them with flowers. Jasmine and rose are now the best-loved, but many flowers including chrysanthemums, marigolds and fruit blossoms have also been used.

The Chinese also changed their brewing methods. They drank boiled cake tea during the Tang dynasty (628–907), later developing powdered green tea whipped until it had a foamy head in the Sung dynasty (960–1127). Steeped tea only became the norm in the Ming dynasty (1368–1644). It was this tea that European merchants of the Renaissance first encountered, and so it was this way of making tea that came to the west.

Tea in Japan

The Japanese also usually drink steeped tea, serving it from lovely pots or buying it from wagons in the street, even glugging it in tins from slot machines. Yet the whipped green tea of the Sung dynasty – 'froth of the liquid jade' Okakura called it – survives in the Japanese tea ceremony, and is still the most prized.

Okakura writes that tea arrived in Japan in 729 when the Emperor Shomu served it to 100 monks to help them stay awake during a four-day reading of Buddhist scriptures. Monks began growing it at their monasteries, and in 1191 the monk Yeisaizenji brought new tea plants and information about the fashionable whipped tea from China, thus shaping the love of tea and the art of making it in Japan.

The legend of Daruma's eyelids

The Japanese myth about the origin of tea shows why it was so invaluable to monks that they planted their own tea gardens.

Daruma, the founder of Zen Buddhism, advocated long hours of contemplation. But one day he fell asleep whilst meditating. He was so horrified by this lapse that he cut off

Daruma

Daruma's actions in the Japanese legend of the origins of tea suggest severity, if not masochism. But today he's the Lucky God and plays a happier role in Japanese life. Daruma dolls, usually red with a black beard and moustache, have just two white circles for eyes. No eyelids! Tradition has it that if you add a black pupil to one eye whilst making a wish, you may get your desire. If so, you celebrate by adding the second pupil. Politicians up for election traditionally fill in one eye, triumphantly drawing the second if they win. Doll-owners whose wishes have not been granted at the end of a year, can burn their doll to show they are on another path to achieving their dreams.

Time management teachers sometimes use paper Daruma dolls. They tell their clients to black in one pupil when they start a task. The doll then sits in a conspicuous spot from where it can silently nag until the work is done, and can be celebrated with the second eye.

his eyelids so that unwanted slumber could never again overwhelm him. Where the eyelids fell, two bushes grew, producing leaves that could be brewed into a stimulating drink – tea – that prevented sleep.

This tale of the miraculous appearance of an aid to spiritual contemplation could not be more different from the Chinese legend of Shen Nung, which highlights the lucky discovery of a delightful and health-giving plant. Arthur Dobrin meditates on the two myths in his poem *The Wine of the Poor*, which celebrates the pleasures of tea:

Which to believe –
The eyelids of a holy man
falling to the earth and sprouting,
or a leaf silently descending into an emperor's cup?
I consider this question sipping
one day Spring Jade,
another
Precious Dew

I pour the queen of camellias,
look out of my window
at the rustling bamboo,
breathe in the steam from a blue cup.
Drink slowly
this exotic brew,
this wine of the poor.

Okakura Kakuzo on Teaism

Quoting a sage who said that its 'delicate bitterness reminded him of the after-taste of good counsel', Okakura Kakuzo emphasises the Japanese link between religion and tea. From the days when early Zen Buddhist monks gathered before the image of Bodhi-Dharma to drink tea from a single bowl, Okakura traces Japanese Teaism:

> *A cult founded on the adoration of the beautiful among the sordid facts of everyday existence ... a worship of the Imperfect ... a tender attempt to accomplish something possible in this impossible thing we know as life. ... It is the noble secret of laughing at yourself, calmly yet thoroughly, and is thus humour itself, the smile of philosophy. All genuine humourists may in this sense be called tea philosophers – Thackeray for instance, and of course Shakespeare.*

Most fundamentally, says Okakura, Teaism focuses on the significance of the smallest incidents: 'Those who cannot feel the littleness of great things in themselves are apt to overlook the greatness of little things in others.'

Japanese tea ceremony

Cups of tea swigged off throughout the day can have no such effect, nor can the happy bustle of an English tea-time. But the Japanese tea ceremony *cha-no-yu* ritualises tea-drinking, focusing the mind on every utensil, every step, every gesture.

Traditionally, it occurs in a small tea house. Guests enter via a winding path and a low door that emphasises its separation from the everyday world. They find themselves alone as Kakuzo explains:

> *The host will not enter the room until all the guests have seated themselves and quiet reigns with nothing to break the silence save the note of the boiling water in the iron kettle. The kettle sings well, for pieces of iron are so arranged in the bottom to produce a peculiar melody in which one may hear the echoes of a cataract muffled by clouds, of a distant sea breaking among the rocks, a rainstorm sweeping through a bamboo forest, or of the soughing of pines on some faraway hill.*

The host wipes each utensil with prescribed gestures. The boiling water is poured on *matcha*, a powdered green tea. The stirrer must click just once on the side of the bowl. The host whisks the tea with a bamboo whisk, then turning the cups to their loveliest side presents them to the guests. After drinking every drop, they must ask to examine the cups and utensils and praise their beauty. They may also speak of religion or art, but not of frivolities. The only food served is bean-paste sweets confected to reflect the season:

pink plum-blossom shapes in spring, for example, peach shapes in summer, chestnuts in autumn, green pine-needles in winter.

Describing the ceremony as performed by the early teamasters, Okakura calls it both an 'oasis' – suggesting that it relieves the difficulties of everyday life – and an 'improvised drama ... woven about the tea, the flowers and the paintings' – suggesting it refocuses and clarifies the mind.

The tea ceremony could last up to four hours. Today, it is shorter – a relief to westerners unaccustomed to sitting on their knees. Often it is performed at home, usually by women who have taken classes in *cha-no-yu* and *ikebana* – the art of arranging flowers. Japanese hotels offer it to visitors, while restaurants catering to businessmen have geisha tea ceremonies, where silken kimonos evoke the seasons and porcelain cups brighten the Zen original.

It can all seem fantastical to westerners, but in a melancholy tone Okakura encourages us to think again:

> *When we consider how small after all the cup of human enjoyment is, how soon overflowed with tears, how easily drained to the dregs in our quenchless thirst for infinity, we shall not blame ourselves for making so much of a tea-cup. Mankind has done worse. In the worship of Bacchus we have sacrificed too freely; and we have transfigured the gory image of Mars. Why not consecrate ourselves to the queen of Camellias, and revel in the warm stream of sympathy that flows from her altar?*

Beyond China

By the time Okakura wrote those words in 1906, the British had long revelled in the stream of sympathy flowing from tea. Like the Japanese, they first got tea from China, but unlike the Japanese, they could not grow their own. And this was frustrating, the more so as Britain developed from one of many Renaissance countries vying for trade with the east into the world's most powerful and prideful Nineteenth-Century empire.

The problem was that the Chinese had never been accommodating where trade was concerned. They confined European merchants to ports on the southern coast. They refused to share their secrets, so Europeans knew nothing of how tea was grown and produced. They did not even know that green tea and black tea came from the same plant. Nor did they know how to make the translucent porcelain cups so perfect for drinking it. The Chinese were no less technologically advanced than the early traders – perhaps more so – and their country was so large that they had little need of many European goods. The woollen textiles, which had made England prosperous in the Middle Ages and remained a trade staple, had little charm for the Chinese of hot southern ports. What they mostly wanted was silver and gold.

The East India Company

The East India Company, founded in 1600, had the monopoly on all trade from the East, and when tea came into England, it was their ships that brought it. By the early Eighteenth Century tea had replaced spices and silk as their most important cargo. By 1760 they were carrying 4.5 million tons a year into Britain.

How was it to be paid for? It was impossible to pay for it all in precious metals. So the East India Company began growing opium in India and exporting it to China. This trade prospered, as the drug trade still does, with laws being passed but not heeded, and the Chinese government taking obstreperous action that outraged Britain.

By the Nineteenth Century, the East India Company had conquered about half of India. Its members were fabulously wealthy. Sir Oliver Surface in Richard Brinsley Sheridan's play *The School for Scandal* was one. In disguise, he reminds his nephew Joseph that he had sent him 'bullion, rupees'. The sententious and lying Joseph denies it: 'No, no; a few presents now and then – china, shawls, congou tea.'

Sir Oliver is not duped, but in William Makepeace Thackeray's *Vanity Fair* Joseph Sedley, who had spent twelve years in the East India Company's employ and returned like 'all Indian nabobs ... enormously rich', is easily taken in by Becky Sharp.

Such wealth brought attack. Free traders claimed the Company used its monopoly to keep tea prices artificially high. Others argued against a company operating as both rulers and merchants. In 1834, a new charter forbade trading, and established the Company as effectively the British government in India. Now, deprived of its China tea business, the Company turned its attention to growing tea in India.

Learning to grow tea in India

It was not a new thought. Combing the Himalayas for exotic plants was a favourite exploit of Nineteenth-Century botanists. In the 1820s, Robert Bruce, a British agent in Assam, then newly colonised, reported seeing people chewing leaves he recognised as tea. The government had paid little attention. But as British and Chinese sparring over opium increased – leading eventually to the 1839–1842 Opium Wars – a tea committee was set up to grow tea in Assam. By 1839 G.G. Sigmond was telling the Royal Botanical Society:

> *A discovery has been made of no less importance that the hand of Nature has planted the [tea] shrub within*

the bounds of the wide dominions of Great Britain: a discovery which must materially influence the destinies of nations.

However, it took years to establish tea successfully in Assam. The first would-be growers had little faith in the Assamese plants, so they tried to grow seeds smuggled from China. These languished in Assam or hybridised with native tea to form a tea variety that growers now regard as a nuisance.

Once they realised that the Assamese plant, now called *Camellia sinensis* var. *assamica*, naturally suits local conditions perfectly, they had to learn to process its leaves. The Chinese had kept this a mystery, so Chinese workers had to be brought to Assam. Indian workers also came to cultivate and pick the tea. Hired by 'coolie catchers' who forced them to sign seven-year contracts that effectively enslaved them, they died in their thousands on the long journey up the Brahmaputra river. Tropical diseases also killed many British entrepreneurs, who, with attractive government land leases, hoped to make a fortune in tea. Even before they could plant the land, they had to clear it, which meant catching and training wild elephants to uproot and shift trees.

With all this, Assamese tea lurched through boom and bust cycles. In 1870 90 per cent of Britain's tea was still Chinese, but Assamese tea was poised for take-off. By 1900, Britain imported only 10 per cent of its tea from China, and Hankow exported no tea for the first time on record. Britain's tea now came from India, mostly Assam, but also from Ceylon, now Sri Lanka, where tea plantations had been developed on the Assamese model after a blight ruined its traditional coffee crop in 1869. The climate was perfect for tea, and the country is now renowned for the brisk teas so beloved in Britain.

Persuading Indians to drink tea

With so many people drinking Indian tea, big tea companies created packets and advertisements that emphasised its origins by portraying Indian tea pickers or turbaned Indian servants balancing tea-trays. But few Indians except those who worked closely with the British drank it. Compared to the vast population, the number of tea drinkers was minuscule. So when the Indian Tea Association began to encourage Indians to sample tea in 1901, they were promoting a foreign beverage: notwithstanding the Himalayan origins of the plant and the thousands of Indians who laboured in its growth, the cultivation and drinking of Indian tea was a British project undertaken with Britain's needs in mind.

The Association provided tea in offices, and then during the First World War, in mines and cotton mills. They set up small-time businessmen as *chai wallahs* – tea blokes – by providing kettles and tea so they could sell it at railway stations. As workers took to tea, the Tea Association moved into homes, sending demonstrators house-to-house to teach the art of making it. By the 1930s, they had tea shops in the large cities. In the country they enticed villagers to drink tea by showing free films – then a new phenomenon in India – during which they served cups of tea.

Taking tea Indian style

As Indians took tea to their hearts, they adapted it to their tastes. In a country that adds spices to all food, spicing tea with cardamom, ginger, cloves, nutmeg, cinnamon and other spices was an obvious step, and the Indian love of milk and yoghourt made the addition of milk as natural to them as it was to the British. Sugar, too, is popular. So Indians created their own *masala chai* – sweet milky tea infused with spices.

Indians who came in contact with the British picked up the habit of having biscuits or cakes with their tea. But they complemented them with savoury snacks. In Kiran Desai's *Inheritance of Loss* the cantankerous judge complains when there are only Marie biscuits for tea. He would have liked scones and cheese straws, but settles for chocolate pudding when the cook claims to have nothing else on hand. Terrorists are harder to satisfy, however. When they invade the house a short time later, they demand pakoras and the cook, despite earlier protests about food shortages, manages to rustle up the vegetables, chickpea flour and oil needed to make them (recipe pp. 160–1).

Anita Desai uses this Indian preference for a combination of sweet and savoury tea-time foods to show the strains between Uma and her parents in *Feasting and Fasting*. They complain about her failure to marry, yet use her as an unpaid servant:

> *They look out on the shimmering heat of the afternoon as if the tray with tea, with sweets, with fritters, will materialize and come swimming out of it – to their rescue.*

Worn down by their demands and unable to fight back directly, Uma tries to limit her burdens. She hopes that a savoury something will satisfy them, announcing: 'Fritters for tea. Do you want sweets as well?' They accept the fritters happily when it's just the family at home, but when they meet the parents of Uma's prospective husband, they make sure to do the proper Indian thing and offer both savoury samosas and sweet barfi.

Other tea-growing countries

Today, many countries grow tea. Kenya's mountains, bathed in warm rain-bearing winds from Lake Victoria, have the perfect tea climate. A few small-holders planted it in the early Twentieth Century, and now its tea gardens are so productive that it is the third largest producer in the world.

Tea is also grown in Malawi, Tanzania, Ethiopia and other African countries, where its development was speeded in the Twentieth Century by colonial governments that had learned from the experience of introducing tea to India and Ceylon. Indonesia, South America and over forty other countries also grow tea. In England, it is grown at Tregothnan Estate on the River Fal in Cornwall.

China and India jockey to be the world's largest producer, but since Indians now drink 70 per cent of their crop, Kenya is the world's leading exporter, followed by Sri Lanka. Because of its great size and the production of tea on small farms as well as large plantations, China produces the biggest variety of teas. As for English tea, it is among the world's most expensive. Fortnum and Mason's catalogue recently offered Tregothnan Black at £1,500 per kilo.

Chapter 2

Tea in Britain

> *Cheering the whole land from the palace to the cottage, only by slow and resistless efforts of time and its own virtues.*
>
> Isaac D'Israeli

The Pepyses try tea

On September 25th, 1660, Samuel Pepys wrote in his diary 'I did send for a cup of tea (a China drink) of which I had never drunk before'. He loved novel experiences and tea was new, fashionable, expensive and unobtainable in Britain until 1657, when Thomas Garway advertised it for sale at his coffee house.

The first coffee house had opened in Oxford in 1650, when coffee arrived from Arabia. Like coffee, tea came from a far country; it was drunk hot, and it was not alcoholic: it was an obvious addition to the coffee-house stock-in-trade. Owners introduced it by advertisements such as this from 1658:

> *That excellent and by all Physicians approved China Drink called by the Chineans Tcha, by other Nations Tay, alias Tee, is sold at the Sultaness Head, a Cophee House, in Sweetings Rents, by the Royal Exchange London.*

Echoing Chinese tradition and presaging the health benefits of tea established by modern researchers, Garway's

1660 advertisement claimed tea could see off ailments ranging from headache and giddiness to 'Colds, Dropsies and Scurveys'. In addition:

> *It strengtheneth the Memory, it overcometh superfluous Sleep ... and expelleth Infections.*

Garway sold tea from 'sixteen to fifty shillings a pound' – expensive considering that Pepys paid only two shillings for dinner in a tavern. He mentions tea on only two further occasions, both medical. He drank it to ward off plague in 1665, and in 1669 he recorded: 'Home and found my wife making of tea; a drink which Mr Pelling the poticary tells her is good for her cold and defluxions' – probably a runny nose.

Catherine of Braganza and other tea-drinking queens

While people may have tried tea for their health, it caught on because they enjoyed it – and because it was fashionable. Tea had arrived early in Portugal, a pioneer of trade with China, so when Charles II married the Portuguese princess Catherine of Braganza in 1662, she brought her love of tea with her. Seeing Catherine drink tea with her ladies, other ladies naturally wanted to taste it, and so the custom spread.

Drinking tea was a major innovation because everyone, from the monarch to the poorest labourers, drank beer at every meal, consuming on average three litres per person a day. Tea was destined to take over from beer, especially among the middle classes. While Catherine helped establish it in England, her sister-in-law Mary of Modena, wife to James II, introduced it to Scotland by serving it at the

Palace of Holyroodhouse in 1680. Queen Anne was also a tea drinker, as Alexander Pope – who pronounced tea 'tay' – noted in 1711 when he saluted her in *The Rape of the Lock*:

> *Here thou great Anna, whom three realms obey*
> *Doth sometimes counsel take, and sometimes tea.*

Her favourite tea was bohea, a black tea (pronounced bo-hay), which she drank cold with a shot of Bols.

What's in a name?

The Chinese words for tea *ch'a* and *t'e* are parents to the word for tea in most languages. The Portuguese were based in Canton and they brought the Cantonese *ch'a* to Europe, while the Dutch, whose port was Amoy, brought the Amoy form *t'e*. *T'e* became tea in English, at first often pronounced (and spelled) tay. From *ch'a* English gets the colloquial char. Other languages fall into the *ch'a* lineage or the *t'e*:

CH'A	T'E
• Arabic – *Shay*	Dutch – *Thee*
• Greek – *Tsae*	French – *Thé*
• Hindi – *Chah*	German – *Tee*
• Portuguese – *Chá*	Irish – *Tae*
• Russian – *Chai*	Italian – *Tè*
• Serbo-Croatian – *Čaj*	Spanish – *Té*
• Turkish – *Çayi*	Welsh – *Te*

Polish goes its own way. Tea is *herbata*.

Sole empress of the tea table in Congreve's plays

Women could not enjoy tea at coffee houses, which were male-only resorts, so they drank it at home. By 1700, less than fifty years after tea had arrived in Britain, William Congreve suggested that being able to offer tea to friends was a wife's prerogative. In his play *The Way of the World* Millamant refuses to 'dwindle into marriage' with Mirabell until he meets her demand:

> *To be sole Empress of my Tea-table, which you must never presume to approach without first asking leave.*

Mirabell acquiesces with provisos that distinguish the tea-table realm from the coffee house:

> *To your dominion of the Tea-table I submit ... But restrain yourself to native and simple Tea-table drinks, as Tea, Chocolate, Coffee. And likewise to Genuine and Authoriz'd Tea-table talk – such as mending of Fashions, spoiling Reputations, railing at absent Friends, and so forth – and that on no account encroach upon the men's prerogative and presume to drink healths, or toste fellows; for prevention of which I banish all Auxiliaries to the Tea-Table as Orange Brandy, all Anniseed, Cinnamon, Citron and Barbadoes Waters, together with Ratafia.*

In an earlier Congreve play *The Double Dealer* of 1694, the women were described as 'retired to their tea and scandal'– a put-down that hides the fact that tea (and coffee, too) caught on quickly precisely because people could drink them and still talk intelligently, plan marriages, shred reputations and even transact business – none of which were aided by the vast consumption of alcoholic drinks typical before then. Indeed, men did so much business over tea and coffee that the Bank of England and Lloyd's of London both started as coffee houses. Richard Steele, editor of *The Tatler*, used the Grecian coffee house as his editorial office.

Tea versus coffee

In 1700, London had more coffee houses than any city in Europe. Yet by 1706, when Thomas Twining, founder of the famous tea company, opened Tom's Coffee House on the Strand, he quickly realised that tea was a better venture. By 1717, he had renamed his establishment The Golden Lyon and specialised in selling tea blended to order. Significantly, it always welcomed female customers, including, a century later, Jane Austen.

The business survives in the same location opposite the Royal Courts of Justice, evidence that the English, unlike most Europeans, have long favoured tea over coffee. Tea also won out over chocolate, a drink that also arrived in the 1650s. Okakura Kakuzo, that most confident of tea aficionados, attributed this to inherent superiority, 'It has not the arrogance of wine, the self-consciousness of coffee, nor the simpering innocence of cocoa.'

An economic explanation is that the East India Company had the monopoly on importing tea from China. They also had the ear of the government, and this helped them promote tea rather than coffee, which came from countries of the rival Ottoman Empire.

Another factor explaining the rapid adoption of tea is that the vast consumption of beer required around half of England's grain crop. As the population increased, this was insupportable, so another drink that could be consumed in quantity was essential. Tea worked well for the English palate because, like beer, it has a bitter edge, and the coarse brown sugar used to sweeten it in the

Eighteenth Century may have added some beery flavour notes. Notably, when steady supplies of Assamese tea arrived in the mid-Nineteenth Century, its malty flavour – reminiscent of the maltiness of beer – appealed so much that it soon replaced Chinese tea in popular preference.

Dr. Johnson: tea at all hours

Eighteenth-Century doctors battled over the question of how much tea should be drunk. Many swore by it, suggesting that no amount was too much; others thundered against its dangers. John Lettsom, for example, thought it led to alcoholism because 'As tea enfeebles, the trembling hand reaches for the bottle'. William Ellis, author of *The Country Housewife and Family Companion* (1750), decided that 'tea breeds asthma and stoppage at the stomach' after reporting on a young woman who blamed her 'dead palsy' on drinking too much tea when she was a lady's maid.

These problems never afflicted Dr. Samuel Johnson, though he drank tea incessantly. While Jonas Hanway was claiming in his 1756 *Essay on Tea* that tea was 'pernicious to health, obstructing industry, and impoverishing the nation', Johnson was insisting, 'You cannot make the tea so fast as I can gulp it down'. The artist Sir Joshua Reynolds noted that Johnson had drunk eleven cups of tea in one evening. Calling for another cup to make it a round dozen, Johnson replied: 'Sir, I did not count your glasses of wine, why, then, should you number my cups of tea?'

His biographer James Boswell averred:

> *No person ever enjoyed more the infusion of that fragrant leaf than Johnson. The quantities that he drunk of it at all hours were so great that his nerves must have been uncommonly strong, not to have been relaxed by such intemperate use.*

The potential for relaxed nerves suggests that Boswell shared the misgivings about the effects of tea.

Jane Austen's Regency breakfast and after-dinner tea

Johnson cheerfully asserted that he was one 'who with tea welcomes the morning'. As did Jane Austen. She bought the household's tea on visits to London, writing to her brother there, 'We began our China tea three days ago, and I find it very good'.

A letter to her sister Cassandra suggests what she liked to eat with her tea: 'You know how interesting the purchase of a sponge-cake is to me' (see recipe p. 148). Tea was so routine at their breakfast that when her wealthy brother was expected, she reminded Cassandra that 'Edward always drinks coffee for breakfast'.

Tea is the breakfast drink in *Sense and Sensibility*, and in *Northanger Abbey* Catherine Morland is bowled over by breakfast tea served from General Tilney's Staffordshire china.

Jane Austen's characters also drink tea in the evening, after the late-afternoon dinner typical of her era. After eating ladies whiled away an hour or so in the drawing room, while the men had a last drink before joining them for tea, cakes, conversation, cards and music. The arrival of after-dinner tea thus signalled the start of the evening's fun. In Austen's unfinished *The Watsons* Mary and Emma Watson find time hanging heavily as they look forward to leaving for an 8 o'clock ball:

> *The entrance of the tea things at 7 o'clock was some relief . . . and luckily Mr. and Mrs. Edwards always drank a dish extraordinary, and ate an additional muffin when they were going to sit up late, which lengthened the ceremony almost to the wished for moment.*

(Muffin recipe, p. 131.) In *Mansfield Park* also, tea cannot come too soon for Fanny Price, who is longing to escape Henry Crawford, who has just asked her to marry him. Distressed by this unwelcome idea, she wants to flee to her room, but etiquette forbids leaving until after tea:

> *She could have hardly kept her seat any longer had it not been for the sound of approaching relief, the very sound she had been waiting for, and long thinking it strangely delayed. The solemn procession ... of the tea board, urn and cake bearers made its appearance and delivered her. ... Mr Crawford was forced to move away.*

In *Emma* Mr. Woodhouse, ever fearful of ventures beyond his own doors, remembers the rule of not departing before tea when he advises Emma to leave the Coles' party as soon as it is served. He forgets that this would deprive her of the evening's pleasures. Luckily, Mr. Weston notes that going early would hurt the Coles' feelings. She is allowed to stay, and has a good time speculating on the romantic interests of the other guests, playing the piano, listening to Jane Fairfax play better and dancing country dances. Jane Austen recorded just such a real-life occasion when her niece Anna dined with neighbours, 'A delightful evening ... Syllabub, Tea, Coffee, Singing, Dancing and a Hot Supper at eleven o'clock'.

Sinful possets in the Eighteenth Century

Like Jane Austen and her characters, the Reverend Balwhidder in John Galt's fictional chronicle of life in Eighteenth-Century Scotland, *Annals of the Parish*, writes: 'We had tea for our breakfast in the morning at the Manse, as well as in the afternoon.' Though proud of this refined custom, he took a while to overcome his disapproval of tea. Describing a group of women enjoying it outdoors, he says:

> *Just as the witches of lang syne had their sinful possets they made their tea for common in a pint stoup ... for there were but few had cups and saucers.*

He suspects their tea is laced with cognac, and for sure he knows both were smuggled. In his account of 1761 he writes:

> *It was in that year that the great smuggling trade corrupted all the west coast. ... The tea was going like the chaff, the brandy like well-water ... [there were] battles between the smugglers and the King's men, both by sea and land.*

The profits from smuggling led to extravagance – which equalled sinfulness in Reverend Balwhidder's mind. He warned his parishioners that the money would disappear 'like snow off the dyke', but to no avail: 'We had no less than three contested bastard bairns upon our hands at one time.'

Smugglers

The rewards of smuggling tea were no fiction. Historians believe that probably half the tea in Eighteenth-Century Britain lacked a Customs officer's blessing. Nobody was much bothered except the East India Company, which had huge inventories of unsold tea, and the Reverend Balwhidder who, in one year alone, preached sixteen sermons on the text 'Render Unto Caesar the Things That Are Caesar's'. In contrast, Parson Woodforde, whose parish was near Norfolk, showed no disapproval in his diary entry for March 29, 1777:

> *Andrews the smuggler brought me this night about 11 o'clock a bag of Hyson Tea about 6 Pd weight. He frightened me a little by whistling under the Parlour window just as we were going to bed. I . . . paid him for the tea at 10/6 per Pd.*

With tea taxed at 119 per cent, smugglers bought it from East India Company officers, who could import merchandise on their own account. It was the perfect contraband: easy to ferry ashore and easy to sell because everyone wanted it. Smuggling tea was such a money-maker that interference led to Mafia-style revenges. Yet it disappeared overnight in 1784 when the government realised it could stop it by cutting the tea tax by 12½ per cent and taxing windows to make up the difference in revenue.

The Boston Tea Party

With smuggling cutting into its profits, the East India Company proposed to sell tea directly to America – apparently a win-win idea. The East India Company would dispose of its vast stores of tea and claw back some profits, and with a modest 3d per pound tax on tea in America – much less than the tax in Britain – the government would also be in the money. Theoretically, the Americans would get cheaper tea by buying it directly rather than, as previously, from middlemen who shipped it from England. In practice, Americans smuggled much of their tea – a thrifty habit defended by the principle of not paying taxes without representation in the government that imposed them. This principle doomed the stratagem of selling tea direct to America.

In 1773 the *Dartmouth* sailed into Boston loaded with tea. Customs officers finished the paperwork for off-loading its cargo so it could not legally depart laden with it. But Bostonians refused to pay the tax and set a guard over the *Dartmouth* and three other tea ships to prevent their cargoes coming ashore. To break this stalemate, Francis Rotch, the American owner of two of the ships, asked the American-born governor Thomas Hutchinson for permission to leave with the tea. Hutchinson refused. Now fearing that the tea would be landed, members of the Sons of Liberty, a group of Bostonians fiercely opposed to the British control of the American colonies, disguised themselves as Mohawk Indians and boarded the ships. Three hours later, they had thrown 342 chests of tea into the harbour. Best known as the Boston Tea Party, it was in fact, the Boston tax rebellion. Ralph Waldo Emerson summarised the event in a poem called *Boston*:

The cargo came! And who could blame
If Indians seized the tea,
And, chest by chest, let down the same
Into the laughing sea?
For what avail the plow or sail,
If land, or life, or freedom fail?

The tea-dumping example was soon repeated in New York. When Britain responded with punitive laws, the resentments against its rule grew, leading to the First Continental Congress to plan resistance – a meeting that led to the Declaration of Independence in 1776.

Chinese porcelain and English china

East India Company tea ships also carried Chinese porcelain teaware. Being both heavy and waterproof, porcelain provided ballast in the bottom while tea occupied watertight holds higher up. The sheer quantity of porcelain that arrived in England is hard to grasp except, perhaps, through such orders as this to just one East India Company ship in 1709:

Forty tons of China ware of the sorts undermentioned, or if the quantity should amount to more, yet bring it as being heavy goods:

50,000 teacups of several patterns
50,000 saucers to ditto
5,000 teapots with straight spouts
5,000 small deep plates for the teapots
8,000 milk pots
12,000 boats for the teaspoons
2,000 small tea canisters
3,000 sugar dishes
3,000 bowls of about 3 pints

Sugar and milk have never been served in tea in China, so the milkpots, spoon boats and sugar dishes were made solely for export. Lady Russell was clearly thrilled when she discovered milk pots in 1698, writing to her daughter:

Yesterday I met with a little bottle to pour milk out for tea, they call them milk bottles, I was much delighted with them and so put them up for presents to you.

Spoon boats were needed for wet teaspoons, but they disappeared later in the Eighteenth Century, when etiquette demanded putting the spoon into the cup to signal you had had enough.

The saucers were not only receptacles of the cup but drinking vessels too. As recently as the Twentieth Century D.H. Lawrence described Paul Morel's miner father drinking from his saucer in *Sons and Lovers*:

He poured out a saucerful of tea, blew it, and sucked it up through his great black moustache, sighing afterwards. Then he poured out another saucerful and stood his cup on the table. 'My cloth!' said Mrs Morel, putting it on a plate.

Mrs. Morel has more genteel ways than her husband, but drinking from the saucer was not just a working-class habit. It was a way to get tea fast because it cooled quicker in a saucer. Even the denizens of E.F. Benson's Mapp and Lucia novels resort to it, including the wealthy Lucia: 'The rasping beverage rapidly revived Lucia; she drank two cups, the first out of the saucer.'

Showing off the best china

Sets of china have always been prized. On a 1784 visit to England, the Comte de Rochefoucauld noted: 'The drinking of tea ... gives the rich an opportunity to show off their fine possessions: cups, teapots, etc., all made to the most elegant designs.'

General Tilney is typical when he shows off his china to Catherine in Jane Austen's *Northanger Abbey*:

The elegance of the breakfast set forced itself on Catherine's notice ... and luckily it had been the General's choice. He was enchanted by the approbation of his taste, confessed it to be neat and simple, thought it right to encourage the Manufacture of his country; and for his part, to his uncritical palate, the tea was as well flavored from the clay of Staffordshire, as from that of Dresden or Sêve (sic). But this was quite an old set, purchased two years ago. The manufacture was much improved since that time, he had seen some beautiful specimens when last in town, and had he not been perfectly without vanity of that kind, might have been tempted to order a new one.

Staffordshire bone china

When this was written in 1798, Staffordshire-based potteries, led by Spode, had just begun making bone china, a form of porcelain unrivalled for its durability, brilliant finish and the ease of firing and decorating it. The English companies were latecomers to the field compared to the Europeans mentioned by General Tilney: Sêvres and especially Meissen of Dresden, which had unravelled the mystery of making Chinese-style hard-paste porcelain in 1710. But bone china from Spode and its many rivals soon dominated the English market. Most was made in Stoke-on-Trent, an amalgam of six small Staffordshire pottery towns that Arnold Bennett, a native 'Stokie', fictionalised as the Five Towns. In 1908, he described them in *The Old Wives' Tale*:

> *They are unique and indispensable because you cannot drink tea out of a teacup without the aid of the Five Towns; because you cannot eat a meal in decency without the aid of the Five Towns. For this the architecture of the Five Towns is an architecture of ovens and chimneys; for this its atmosphere is as black as mud; for this it burns and smokes all night, so that Longshaw has been compared to hell; for this it is unlearned in the ways of agriculture, never having seen corn except as packing straw and in quartern loaves; for this, on the other hand, it comprehends the mysterious habits of fire and pure sterile earth; for this it lives crammed together in slippery streets ... for this it exists – that you may drink tea out of a teacup and toy with a chop on a plate. All everyday crockery used in the kingdom is made in the Five Towns – all and much besides. ... Even the majestic thought that whenever and wherever in all England a woman washes up, she washes up the product of the district; that whenever and wherever in all England a plate is broken the fracture means new business for the district – even this majestic thought had probably never occurred to either of the girls.*

Elegant economy: tea in Cranford (mid-Nineteenth Century)

The elderly ladies of Mrs. Gaskell's *Cranford* certainly did not ponder the business of Stoke-on-Trent though they owned some of its pretty teacups, as Mary, a young visitor to Cranford notes when describing the elegant economy of their ways:

> *The china was delicate egg shell; the old-fashioned silver glittered with polishing, but the eatables were of the slightest description. ... We none of us spoke of money because the subject savoured of commerce and trade and though some might be poor, we were all aristocratic.*

They were all tactful, too. When Mrs. Forrester entertains in her 'baby house of a dwelling', her maid has to ask the ladies on the sofa to move so she can get the tea tray from underneath; no one raises an eyebrow:

> *Every one took this novel proceeding as the most natural thing in the world ... as if we all believed that our hostess had a regular servants' hall, second table, with housekeeper and steward, instead of one little charity-school maiden, whose short ruddy arms could never have been strong enough to carry the tray upstairs, if she had not been assisted in private by her mistress, who now sat in state, pretending not to know what cakes were sent up, though she knew, and we knew, and she knew that we knew, and we knew that she knew that we knew, that she had been busy all morning making tea bread and sponge cake.*

(Sponge cake recipe, pp. 148–9.) The Honourable Mrs. Jamieson only provides wafer-thin bread and butter and sponge biscuits. Giving more 'was considered "vulgar" (a tremendous word in Cranford)', so when Mrs Jamieson invites everyone to tea:

> *Very delicate was the china, very old the plate, very thin the bread and butter, and very small the lumps of sugar. Sugar was evidently Mrs. Jamieson's favourite economy. I question if the little filigree sugar-tongs, made something like scissors, could have opened themselves wide enough to take up an honest, vulgar good-sized piece; and when I tried to seize two little minnikin pieces at once so as not to be detected in too many returns to the sugar-basin, they absolutely dropped one, with a little sharp clatter, quite in a malicious and unnatural manner.*

Her own practice notwithstanding, Mrs Jamieson discovers an ample appetite when entertained by Miss Betty Barker, definitely not of the Cranford aristocracy, yet tolerated because she had been a lady's maid:

> *Mrs. Jamieson was kindly indulgent of Miss Barker's want of knowledge of the customs of highlife; and to spare her feelings, ate three large pieces of seed-cake with the placid ruminating expression of countenance, not unlike a cow's.*

(Seed-cake recipe, pp. 147–8.) Miss Barker concludes her entertainment with a supper of scalloped oysters, potted lobster, and 'little Cupids made from macaroons soaked in brandy'. Again the ladies 'thought it better to submit graciously' to these, though they 'never ate suppers in general'.

Both Miss Barker and her guests consider she is honoured by their presence at her tea-table, but she is richer than they are because she had worked all her life. This aligns her to the world of the nearby city of Drumble, whose commercial values are among the vulgarities the Cranford ladies think best to ignore. Their silver and china survive from past family affluence, but their tea-time morsels show the narrowness of lives in which cards are 'the most earnest and serious business they ever engaged in'. Mrs. Gaskell loves Cranford too much to pencil this observation in heavy black, but she makes clear that prosperous businesses are not to be scorned. After Miss Matty's pittance disappears in a bank failure, Mary's father, a Drumble businessman, salvages what he can, and sets her up in a little tea business run from her parlour. The grocer helps by directing some of his customers to her on the pretence that she stocks better teas. Mary comments:

> *Expensive tea is a very favourite luxury with well-to-do tradespeople and rich farmers' wives, who turn up their noses at the Congou and Souchong prevalent at many tables of gentility, and will have nothing else than Gunpowder and Pekoe for themselves.*

Tea for all

Mrs. Gaskell knew all about the preferences of 'well-to-do tradespeople' because though she based Cranford on the Cheshire village of Knutsford, where she grew up in the 1830s, she wrote it in the early 1850s, when she lived in Manchester, then at the height of its cotton-making prosperity and her model for Drumble. Manchester's tradespeople could afford whatever tea they fancied, but the factory workers enjoyed tea at least as much. At meal breaks, it restored the energy and concentration needed for keeping an eye on the machines for 12-hour days, and it helped clear the throat of the dust that filled the air.

Even in the Eighteenth Century working people preferred tea. In 1781, Charles Deering described women in Nottinghamshire's textile factories: 'Even a Common Washerwoman thinks she has not had a proper breakfast without Tea and hot buttered white Bread.'

Foreign visitors were amazed that everyone drank tea in Britain. In 1784, the Comte de la Rochefoucauld wrote, 'The humblest peasant has his tea twice a day just like the rich man'. Erik Gustav Geier visiting from Sweden in 1809 described tables in London's streets where 'coal carters and workmen empty their cups of delicious beverage'.

Getting the most from the tea leaves

Coming from coffee-drinking countries, La Rochefoucauld and Geier perhaps did not realise that, unlike coffee, tea can be infused several times. In the process, it could get very wan. When vampires nightly attack Mina Harker in *Dracula*, Bram Stoker could think of no better analogy to her dreadful pallor than 'tea after the teapot had been watered'.

But watered tea was often the best servants could hope for. When the mistress in the drawing room had finished with her teapot, they steeped the leaves again. Jonathan Swift wrote tongue-in-cheek about the hard lot of maids whose mistresses kept their tea in locked canisters, thus:

> *Without which it is impossible for a Waiting-maid to live. For by this means you are forced to buy brown Sugar and pour Water upon the Leaves when they have lost all their Spirit and Taste.*

Charwomen were next in line for used tea leaves. They sold them to dealers, who made 'new tea' by drying them on hot metal plates and mixing them with a few fresh leaves. 'Wrecked' tea from sunken ships was treated the same way.

In the late 1840s, journalist Henry Mayhew, who had sleuthed through London's grey economy to uncover such stratagems for making a few shillings, noted the irony that charwomen actually gathered their own tea:

> *By charwomen and washerwomen a 'nice cup of tea' in the afternoon during their work is generally classed among the*

Milk and Sugar?

Mayhew's charwomen and other workers who loved 'their nice cup of tea' typically drank it with milk and sugar. Both were added to tea early in its British history, though unknown to Chinese tea drinkers.

Why did milk and sugar appeal in Britain? One reason is that they soften the taste, milk especially since it binds the tannins that make tea astringent.

When tea arrived in the Seventeenth Century, both milk and sugar were familiar ingredients in hot drinks such as possets and caudles of warmed wine or beer mixed with sugar, spices and milk. Like these, tea was served hot, so milk and sugar probably seemed obvious additions.

Most significantly, tea itself has no calories, but poor people needed all the calories they could get because they worked hard and often ate meagrely. Drinking tea rather than beer was a nutritional loss to them because beer has nutrients. Even tea-drinking Dr. Johnson wrote 'Tea is a liquor not proper for the lower classes of people because it supplies no strength to labour'. Milk and sugar added a touch of protein and a few calories to make tea more sustaining.

Notably, the imports of sugar kept lockstep with imports of tea – a partnership noted early in the Eighteenth Century when Joseph Addison defined tea as 'The infusion of a China plant sweetened with the pith of an Indian cane'. The cane did not come from India (though India was an early medieval source of sugar), but from Britain's West Indian plantations.

Britons are not alone in enjoying sugar or something sweet with tea. Indians like tea with sugar, and so do Afghans, adding spoon after spoon of it to their guests' tea as a mark of hospitality. Russians prefer jam, served in a little dish and eaten by spoonfuls alternately with sips of tea.

comforts of existence, yet they are the very persons who sell the tea leaves which are to make their much prized beverage. It is curious to reflect also that as tea leaves are used indiscriminately for being re-made into what is considered new tea, what must be the strength of our tea in a few years. Now all housewives complain that twice the quantity of tea is required to make the infusion of the same strength as formerly, and if the collection of tea-leaves continues, and refuse leaves are to be dried and re-dried perpetually, surely we must get to use pounds where we now do ounces.

Ruskin to the rescue: cutting the cost for the poor

Such trickery was only one form of adulteration. Another was making ersatz tea with sloe or hawthorn leaves, either alone or mixed with a little real tea, plus, sometimes, black lead to perk up the colour. Thus, while Jane Austen was paying £1 per pound for tea from Twining's, poor people paid only pennies. Writing of Scotland in 1795, David Davies noted: 'Tea (with bread) furnishes one meal for a whole family every day at no greater expense than about one shilling a week.'

Their tea was undoubtedly adulterated. Another problem for the poor was that they could only afford small amounts at a time, and the mark-up on these made it as costly as the pounds bought by wealthy customers.

The writer John Ruskin, who hated economic theories that prized profit above all else, had a solution. In 1874, he opened Mr. Ruskin's Tea Shop in Marylebone. It had china teapots in the window, and sold tea 'in packets as small as they [the customers] choose to buy' at reasonable prices. The shop failed. Ruskin explained:

The poor only like to buy their tea where it is brilliantly lighted and eloquently ticketed and I resolutely refuse to compete with my neighboring tradesmen either in gas or rhetoric, the patient subdivision of my parcels by two old servants of my mother ... passes little recognised by the uncalculating public.

Cutting the cost: grocery chains

One of Ruskin's 'neighboring tradesmen' was probably Thomas Lipton. He opened his first grocery in Glasgow in 1871 when he was just 23, and, by 1888, he had 300 shops all over Britain. He kept prices low by cutting out the middleman whenever possible. When he visited Ceylon in 1890, he saw a chance to circumvent the merchants who controlled Britain's tea via the London Tea Auction. He snapped up four tea gardens and started producing his own brand of tea.

Lipton believed in advertising, 'When a hen lays an egg it runs around the farmyard squawking. When a duck lays an egg it sits on it quietly. Who buys duck eggs?'

To make sure customers knew about his sources, he sold tea in colourful packets, sealed to show the tea was pure, and blazoned with the slogan 'Straight from the tea gardens to the tea pot'. Companies such as the Cooperative Wholesale Society, Home and Colonial and Maypole were soon selling tea in packets and bringing decent tea within the budget of poor people.

The streamlined methods of growing tea in India supported their innovations. From the shaky start in Assam in the 1830s, tea gardens had been developed in Darjeeling and Nilgiri Hills, as well as in Sri Lanka – then called Ceylon – the name still given to its teas. Applying the methods of the Industrial Revolution that had brought workers out of their small workplaces and into giant factories, India tea growers planted bushes in long rows marching over hillsides and tended by armies of workers. These economies of scale made Indian tea cheaper than Chinese, which was grown on family plots and bought by merchants who needed dozens of suppliers to accumulate a shipload.

Even in rural areas where tea was once rare, it became the essential drink. At a 1913 conference on diet and health, a Welsh medical officer mourned the changes in his country, noting that fifty years previously, people drank milk: 'Now the majority take tea four or five times a day.'

Cutting the cost: Nineteenth-Century clippers

Shipping, too, helped reduce the cost of tea. It took the East Indiamen about 21 months to go to China round the Cape of Good Hope and back to London with tea. But, in 1849, fast American clipper ships were doing the job in 200 days, and selling their new season's tea for premium prices. Britain began building clippers too and, in 1852, the pointedly named British *Challenger* beat the American *Challenge* into London by two days.

Shortly afterwards, the American ships began working the profitable California gold routes, so British clippers ruled the tea trade. These sharp-bowed, skinny-hulled, slant-masted thoroughbreds of the sea caught the public imagination, and betting on which would arrive home first became a seasonal sport. The 1866 race was the most spectacular: ten ships left Fouchow on the same tide on May 28th. The *Taeping*, *Ariel* and *Serica* docked in London on the same tide 99 days later. A dead heat was declared so that the prize was shared between the first two. In 1872, the *Cutty Sark*, built in Dumbarton and named after a character in Robert Burns' *Tam O'Shanter*, left Shanhou with the *Thermopylae*. Two weeks later she lost her rudder. Rather than stop, her captain continued with an improvised rudder. Nonetheless, she was beaten by only a week, after a journey of 122 days. But by this time the clipper trade was already doomed; the 1869 opening of the Suez Canal cut the distance to China, swinging financial advantage to coal-fired steamers.

The cups that cheer but not inebriate

The cumulative effect of all these changes was that even the poorest could drink tea at every meal. Nonetheless, alcohol retained its appeal. Nineteenth-Century reformers hammered away at its abuse, and tea was a major weapon.

Temperance advocates emphasised its warmth and comfort. Quoting William Cowper's *The Task* they called it 'the cups that cheer but not inebriate'. Tea-loving Prime Minister William Gladstone was often pictured taking tea with his wife. In 1882, he told Parliament, 'The domestic use of tea is a powerful champion able to encounter alcoholic drink in a fair field and throw it in a fair fight.'

Dickens on Nineteenth-Century temperance teas

With such encouragement tea parties became a favoured way to wean men from the pub. In *Pickwick Papers* Charles Dickens described Mrs. Weller luring her husband into a chapel for 'a grand tea-drinkin' for a feller they calls their shepherd'. At half-a-crown a head this fundraiser shocks Mr. Weller. He confides in his son Sam:

> *Such goings on Sammy! 'The kiss of peace,' says the shepherd, and then he kissed the women all round, and ven he done, the man with the red nose began. I was just a thinkin' whether I hadn't better begin too – 'specially as there was a wery nice lady a sittin' next to me – ven in comes tea. ... At it they went, tooth and nail. Such a precious loud hymn, Sammy, while the tea was a brewing; such a grace, such eatin' and drinkin' I wish you could a seen the shepherd walkin' into the ham and muffins.*

Mr. Weller is not best pleased at being called a 'miserable sinner' and a 'wessel of wrath' by 'the shepherd', and he detests the side-kick Mr. Stiggins, who leeches Mrs. Weller's money while supping Mr. Weller's pineapple rum. He plans to expose him as a drinker at the Brick Lane Branch of the United Grand Junction Ebenezer Temperance Association, where drinking tea reaches excesses rivalling those of a pub:

'Sammy,' whispered Mr. Weller, 'if some o' these here people don't want tappin' tomorrow morning, I ain't your father. And that's wot it is. Why, this here old lady in front of me is a drownded 'erself in tea.'

'Be quiet, can't you?' murmured Sam.

'Sam,' whispered Mr. Weller, a moment afterwards, in a tone of deep agitation, 'mark my words, my boy. If that 'ere secretary fellow keeps on for only five minutes more, he'll blow himself up with toast and water.'

'Well, let him, if he likes,' replied Sam; 'it ain't no bis'ness of yourn.'

'If this here lasts much longer, Sammy,' said Mr. Weller in the same low voice, 'I shall feel it my duty as a human bein' to rise and address the cheer. There's a young 'ooman on the next form but two, as has drunk nine breakfast cups and a half; and shes a swellin' wisibly before my wery eyes.'

Tea in wartime: the Twentieth Century

The Nineteenth-Century developments that made tea cheap and universal in Britain also made it essential in the two world wars of the Twentieth Century.

Tea had been present in war even earlier. The Duke of Wellington took his own Wedgwood teapot onto the battlefield, explaining to his generals that tea cleared his head. After Waterloo, cartoonists mocked his fondness for tea, showing him drinking it with frumpy Englishwomen. Later, nursing the injured in the Crimean War, Florence Nightingale asked for tea, noting: 'There is nothing yet discovered which is a substitute to the English patient for his cup of tea.'

Siegfried Sassoon agreed. In *Memoirs of a Fox-Hunting Man* he praised the quartermaster for always getting tea to the men returning exhausted from the trenches of the First World War.

Tea was vital warmth, especially when food was short. Diarist Edwin Campion Vaughan recorded in February 1917, 'We had only one meal during the day, and that of bread and bully, but we made tea three times with water from our bottles.' Things got worse. A day later, 'We had no food or water, but Dunham got a large chunk of ice out of a shell-hole behind us, so we had some milkless tea.'

Rationed tea and stratagems for making the most of it

Fortunately the First World War coincided with bumper tea production in Assam, so supplies to the front were good. But in 1916, two years into the war, the government rationed sugar, which was taken in tea by most people. General rationing did not occur until 1918, the year the war ended.

Remembering this and knowing that 70 per cent of Britain's food, including all its tea, came from overseas, the government introduced rationing just four months after the outbreak of the Second World War in 1939. By July 1940, each person got only two ounces of tea per week and, until 1952, the tea ration never exceeded two and a half ounces.

To ensure supplies, the government bought up all surpluses from all tea-exporting countries. (A document declassified in 2007 shows that in 1967, Harold Wilson's government again planned to buy up tea from India and Sri Lanka for stockpiling against the ravages of a nuclear war.) The effect in the Second World War was that canteens, mobile kitchens and the British Restaurants could sell tea at a penny a pint to people on the move. Two soldiers on an interminable train journey in Anthony Powell's *The Valley of Bones* could thus sustain themselves with tea from a platform stall and 'faded, but still beautiful sausage rolls'.

Tea was one of the most coveted comforts of the war. Stratagems were needed to make the most of it. One was to add a pinch of bicarbonate of soda to add astringency and mimic the taste of a strong brew. As for sugar, it was in such demand for cooking, that many gave up using it in tea. Others perhaps followed the Ministry of Food's advice to sweeten tea with beetroot instead of sugar. Imagination qualms at the thought of the taste and colour of the resulting brew.

Lord Woolton, the former maths teacher who became the Minister of Food, devised the rationing system. He advised:

> *Many people make tea by allowing one teaspoonful a head and one for the pot. The teaspoon 'for the pot' is unnecessary. It is equal over the whole population to sixty shiploads a year. We must have those ships to bring munitions.*

Wartime tea-times

Everything needed for afternoon tea was rationed: tea, sugar, butter, flour, jam. Fresh eggs were rare as were the savoury delicacies that filled sandwiches. Elizabeth Bowen describes a particularly dreary tea in *The Heat of the Day*, set in 1942. Stella Rodney and Robert Kelway are visiting his mother and sister Ernestine: both of them self-centred passive aggressives. The party, including Robert's nephew and niece, Peter and Anne, sit down to:

> *Buns, a cut loaf, an uncut cake which had the look of being of long standing, and an inviting pot of damson jam.*

(Recipe for buns, pp. 135–6.) As his sister saws at the loaf, Robert says:

> *'Mrs. Rodney and I forgot about bringing our own butter.' This served to draw Stella's attention to the butter arrangement: each one of the family had his or her own ration placed before his or her plate in a differently coloured china shell. Today was the delusive opening of the rationing week; the results of intemperance, as the week drew on, would be to be judged.*

Ernestine volunteers, 'I would offer you some of my butter ... but that would only make you feel uncomfy.'

Stella realises that eating in London restaurants (which were supplied with food unobtainable to housewives) 'had kept from her many of the realities of the home-front'. Equally used to restaurant eating, Robert spreads alarm and despondency among the children:

> *Robert helped himself to a bun, which he split open in order to spread thickly with damson jam. 'Oh, I say!' expostulated his nephew Peter, speaking for the first time. The girl Anne remarked, 'Do you do that in London? You must use a lot of jam, a most awful lot!'*

Mrs. Kelway slams a final damper on the meal when she announces:

> *We now drink tea only once a day; otherwise we might not have enough for guests. During the week it frequently*

happens that my daughter has hers at the W.V.S., in which case were it not for the children, I should be tempted to do without mine.

After this sally, Robert 'trying to knife the cake', pointedly asks:

'You wouldn't think it was time we bought a new cake?'
'But that one has not been eaten,' objected Ernestine. 'I am sure Mrs. Rodney will take us as she finds us.'
'Happily for Mrs. Rodney, she does not eat cake.'

The stringencies of this tea-time, if not its tensions, were typical.

Tea today

Coffee was so much a minority taste that it was never rationed. Unlike tea, few Eighteenth and Nineteenth-Century writers mention coffee. The 1844 inventory of Charles Dickens' kitchen records a tea set, tea urns, teapots and kettles, but no coffee-making equipment.

But beginning with the espresso bars of the 1950s and 60s, when coffee became the hip drink, its popularity has grown. Instant coffee, easy to make in a mug, boosted it, and so did coffee lovers who publicised the differences between *Arabica* and *robusta* coffee in the 1980s, paving the way for 'serious' coffee in supermarkets and cafés.

As instant coffee found a market among those who didn't want to brew a full pot, tea bags made it easy to make just one cup of tea. It is only in the last couple of decades or so, that most tea-rooms and tea suppliers have re-emphasised the huge range of traditional and artisan teas and the complexity of their flavours. Tea lovers in even the smallest towns can now sample at least a few of the hundreds of kinds of tea, and treat them, as they deserve, with a seriousness akin to that which connoisseurs devote to wine.

Tea remains Britain's favourite drink. The UK imports 140,000 tons of tea a year, enough to make an annual 62 billion cups or three cups a day for everyone over the age of 10. Of this, 96 per cent is made from tea bags and 98 per cent is drunk with milk, which means that a quarter of Britain's milk is consumed in tea. The population of the United Kingdom and Ireland drinks more tea per capita than anyone else, with the Irish beating the British into second place.

CHAPTER 3

Afternoon and Other Tea-times

If you are cold, tea will warm you; if you are too heated, tea will cool you; if you are depressed, tea will cheer you; if you are excited, tea will calm you.

Prime Minister William Gladstone

AFTERNOON tea seems so traditional that it's rather a surprise that Grendel's mother did not sip a sustaining cup or two before her dramatic exploits against Beowulf. But during its early days in Britain, tea was often a morning affair. In 1711, Joseph Addison, Editor of *The Spectator*, promoted it as a chance to read his publication:

I would therefore in a particular manner recommend these my speculations to all well-regulated families that they set apart an hour every morning for tea and bread and butter, and would earnestly advise them for their own good to order this paper to be punctually served up and to be looked upon as a part of the tea equipage.

Tea remains a way to greet the day. The people of the fictional Llaregybb in Dylan Thomas's *Under Milk Wood* wake up to it, with Mrs. Beynon demanding: 'Where's my tea, girl?' The servant Lily answers under her breath: 'Where do you think? In the catbox?' Willy Nilly 'downs his last bucket of brackish tea'; his hens 'grieve for their tea-soaked sops', while Mrs. Willy Nilly 'full of tea to her double-chinned brim' boils the kettles she needs to steam open everyone's mail.

Even those whose late-night exploits kept them in bed all morning had tea to get them started, according to Eighteenth-Century dramatist John Gay:

At noon (the lady's matin hour)
I sip the tea's delicious flower.

Jane Austen and her characters also took tea at breakfast and again after dinner (see p. 33). Afternoon tea was really a Nineteenth-Century invention that did not appear until a quarter of a century after Jane Austen's death in 1817. Looking back to 1842, the actress Frances Kemble recalled:

My first introduction to 'afternoon tea' took place during this visit to Belvoir. ... I do not believe that the now universally-honoured institution of 'five o'clock tea' dates further back than this.

Of course, people often drank a cup of tea in the afternoon before this date. In the Eighteenth-Century *Annals of the Parish* John Galt's Reverend Balwhidder comes courting his third wife in the afternoon just as the servant brings in tea. In 1788, Parson Woodforde's Diary records that Mrs. Davy 'drank Tea here', having shown up uninvited at around five o'clock:

Soon after Mrs. Davy came also Mr. Walker and another young Man by name Viol, both almost wet thro' and they drank Tea also here on their road from Norwich homewards, so that my House was more like an Inn.

Sinking feelings

The difference between a cup of tea sipped in an Eighteenth-Century afternoon and the mid-Nineteenth-Century afternoon tea was the myriad of charming eatables that make afternoon tea so entrancing. Anna, seventh Duchess of Bedford, is credited with making these fashionable when she asked her servants to bring sandwiches and cake with tea to ward off the 'sinking feeling' that afflicted her as afternoon drew to its close.

The Duchess's sinking feelings are not surprising. Dinner had long been a moving target. In Queen Elizabeth I's day it came at midday. In the late Eighteenth Century it had moved to about 3pm – later in wealthier circles. The Brontës had dinner at two and tea in the early evening in the first half of the Nineteenth Century, but in affluent homes, dinner had already slid to later in the day. Jane Austen's family dined at 3.30pm when they lived in Hampshire in the 1790s, but by 1806, when they took a house in Southampton, they ate dinner at 5pm. The Bennett family in *Pride and Prejudice* dine at four. Jane's rich brother Edward dined at 6.30pm. In her unfinished novel *The Watsons* the impoverished sisters Emma and Eliza dine at three, while the aristocratic Osbornes eat at eight. This time became the norm in the Nineteenth Century. People were hungry well beforehand. Afternoon tea at four or five filled the gap.

Alluring food

In days when tea followed dinner, little cakes or biscuits accompanied it, just as today's after-dinner coffee comes with petits fours or chocolates. But since people had just eaten a large meal, the tea-time delicacies were slight and writers rarely noted them. In contrast, the food served with afternoon tea has always charmed, and novelists and playwrights have typified their characters by what they eat at tea.

In *North and South* Mrs. Gaskell evokes the modest though alluring tea prepared by the Hales and glimpsed by John Thornton as he enters:

> *Behind the door was another table decked out for tea, with a white tablecloth on which flourished the cocoa-nut cakes, and a basket piled with oranges and ruddy American apples, heaped on leaves.*

The cocoa-nut (coconut) cakes (recipe, pp. 138–9) are a speciality of the house made by Margaret Hale and the servant. Such family recipes were often secret – which intensified their appeal. In *The Last September* Elizabeth Bowen recalls a family who served a 'chocolate cake made by a charm', (see recipe pp. 149–50) and her story *Sunday Afternoon* has another chocolate cake (or perhaps the same one?) 'for which the Vesey cook had been famous since Henry was a boy'. In Molly Keane's *Good Behaviour* the Crowhurst twins make 'wonderful potted fish (it's their secret still)'. Aroon St Charles finds 'their fish paté sandwiches irresistible' (see recipe pp. 157–8). Equally captivating is the tea served to her bedridden father:

> *Though he did not eat much of them, Papa liked sandwiches and tiny scones, and medlar jelly, iced orange cakes and ginger cake. Mummie of course ate nothing, so there was usually enough for me.*

Indeed, novels of country house life in Ireland are packed with lavish teas. (Recipes for scones and orange cake, pp. 137–8 and 150–1.) In *The Last September*, Elizabeth Bowen's evocation of the last months of British rule, Mrs. Vermont, wife of an English army officer, seriously tucks in:

Mrs Vermont ate more hot cakes than she cared to remember because they were so good and nobody seemed to notice. She went on to chocolate cake, and then to orange layer cake, to which she returned again and again. An idea she had had, that one should not eat very much when invited out, languished; she finished up with a plate of raspberries.

That plate of raspberries means there are not enough to go around. Elizabeth Bowen, who loved entertaining at her homes in Ireland and England, describes Mrs. Vermont from the point of view of the watchful hostess who knows greed when she sees it. She smiles wryly at Mrs. Vermont's obliviousness, yet not without letting the careful reader see it is an indictment of her country, still, largely oblivious to Ireland's tinder-box situation.

Supplying Queen Victoria's tea table

Tea-time cakes like those Mrs. Vermont gobbled are legion: fruit cake, seed-cake, walnut cake, genoa cake, lemon cake as well as various sponge and chocolate cakes plus Victoria sandwich. The latter was named after Queen Victoria. In 1897, the anonymous author of *The Private Life of the Queen* explained that 'The refreshing cup of tea has ever ranked high in the Royal favour'. Her servant John Brown boiled outdoor kettles to make tea while she and her daughters sketched moorland scenes, and tea-time fare followed her around the country:

It is principally to supply the Queen's tea table that the confectionery cooks are kept busy all year round at Windsor, for wherever the Court may be there must follow a large supply of cakes. Among the favourites of the Queen which are carefully packed in small tin boxes and sent to the Court four times a week are chocolate sponges, plain sponges, wafers of two or three shapes, 'langues de chat', biscuits and

> *drop cakes of all kinds, tablets, 'petits fours', princess and rice cakes, pralines, almond sweets, and a large quantity of mixed sweets.*

Bread and butter before cake

Before eating such sweet treats, thinly sliced bread, already buttered, was the thing to start it with. Children certainly had to get through a slice or two to qualify for cakes:

> *Always bread and butter first: they had been told that so many times that it had the finality of a text of Scripture. But Mr. Herring, who was the eldest present and ought to have set a good example, began with the little cakes, picking up and examining each one closely before disposing of it in two bites. However, while there were still a few left, Mrs. Herring placed bread and butter on his plate, and handed him the lettuce meaningfully.*

So writes Flora Thompson, recalling her late-Nineteenth-Century childhood in *Lark Rise to Candleford*. Preferences for cakes and biscuits often meant that the bread and butter was left over to be turned into bread and butter pudding or curly jinny the next day. As well as bread there might be buns, and in winter, hot, buttery toast, muffins or crumpets.

Scones: newcomers to England

Scones are recorded as special-occasion fare in their native Scotland from the Sixteenth Century. Unlike the oat breads usually eaten there, they were made of wheat flour so they were soft. Robert Burns called them 'souple (supple) scones, the wale (choicest) of food' (recipe pp. 137–8). But scones did not become a mainstay of English tea-times until the Twentieth Century. Mrs. Beeton does not give a recipe in her 1861 *Book of Household Management*, and the 1895 tea menu at Harrods did not offer them, though they appeared on its new restaurant menu in 1911. By 1924, when May Sinclair published her novel *The Cure of Souls*, Canon Chamberlain clearly agrees with Burns, 'He had a vision of small delicate home-made scones, hot-buttered'.

Many other regional specialities also star at tea-time: treacle scones and drop scones in Scotland, teacakes and curd tarts in Yorkshire, saffron bread and buns in Cornwall, fruit breads such as bara brith in Wales and tea brack in Ireland. Regional griddle cakes include potato cakes from Ireland and the north-west of England, singing hinnies from the north-east, pikelets from the Midlands, while Eccles cakes, Chorley cakes and Banbury cakes are curranty cousins from different towns. As for gingerbread, Ashbourne in Derbyshire and Grasmere in Cumbria are only two of many towns that have their own traditional kinds.

Sandwiches complement this sweet array with savoury fillings that can be as perfectly quiet as cucumber or as sumptuous as smoked salmon or the paté served to Rosie, the Kentish barmaid adored by all men in Somerset Maugham's *Cakes and Ale*. Having eloped with the most vigorous (but rascally) man in the village, she ends her days in New York luxury:

> *The ... maid brought in an elaborate tea with paté sandwiches and candy and little knives and forks and tiny napkins. It was all very neat and smart.*
>
> *'That's one thing I've never been able to do without – my tea,' said Rosie, helping herself to a hot buttered scone. 'It's my best meal, really, though I know I shouldn't eat it. My doctor keeps on saying to me: "Mrs. Iggulden, you can't expect to keep your weight down if you will eat half a dozen cookies at tea." But what I say is: A little of what you fancy does you good.' ... She gave me a smile, and I had a sudden*

inkling that, notwithstanding the marcelled hair and the powder and the fat, Rosie was the same as ever.

Rosie's tea-tray had no fruit on it, but, like savoury sandwiches, fruit complements cakes and scones. It usually appears as jam, but summer brings the luxury of strawberries or raspberries and cream as the high point of tea. Almost any fruit is welcome. When schoolgirls Sandy and Jenny have tea in Muriel Spark's *The Prime of Miss Jean Brodie,* their special treat was canned pineapple cubes with cream, while in E.F. Benson's *Queen Lucia,* Lucia tempts her guests with peaches and four kinds of sandwiches.

Voluptuous teas to high tea

The lovely peaches are typical of the 'pleasant tea parties for eight with sessions of bridge before and after' that punctuate life in Benson's Mapp and Lucia novels, especially when Lucia is the hostess:

Voluptuous teas were the rule, after which you wanted no more than little bits of things, a cup of soup, a slice of cold tart, or a dished-up piece of fish or toasted cheese, supping modestly from a tray.

Tea could replace dinner. Indeed, afternoon tea lends itself to amplifications. In Somerset Maugham's *Of Human Bondage,* Philip's clergyman uncle always has an egg at Sunday tea 'to fortify him for the evening service'. Ham and other cold meats were also favourite reinforcements. Salads could appear too. In *Lark Rise to Candleford* Mr. Herring rolls up lettuce leaves and dips them into salt. In a gentler scene from D.H. Lawrence's *Sons and Lovers* the old lady who serves Paul and Clara's tea in her Derbyshire cottage pops out to her garden for fresh-pulled radishes and a cucumber.

Tea gowns

In 1878, a writer in the *Royal Exchange* magazine huffed and puffed:

> *Ladies, who a few years ago would have considered the idea appalling calmly array themselves in the glorified dressing robe known as a 'tea gown'.*

This shock-horror carried no weight. Women loved tea gowns. Unlike the tight-skirted, boned and bustled dresses of the late Nineteenth Century, tea gowns came in light fabrics ornamented at the neck and shoulders with frothy laces and frivolous frills. Women wore these comfortable dresses to entertain friends to tea, and, also for at-home dinner. But etiquette writers instructed 'One does not go out to dine in a tea-gown except in the house of a member of one's family or a most intimate friend'.

In the 1920s Miss Mapp inaugurates a new season of tea and bridge parties typical of E.F. Benson's Mapp and Lucia novels wearing a kingfisher-blue tea gown:

> *She had not anticipated that artificial light would cast a pale (though not ghastly) reflection from the vibrant blue on her features... She did not look ill – she was satisfied as to that – simply gorgeous and a little wan.*

Unfortunately, her friend Diva wears the same gown, and when Mapp is persuaded that the dress could take a crimson-lake dye, Diva has the same idea inspired by the same dressmaker, so the next party finds them both casting ruddy glows from red gowns. But neither kingfisher-blue nor crimson-lake would have been right for a tea gown. In rebellion against textiles brilliantly coloured with the new aniline dyes of the Nineteenth Century, the ideal tea gown was light in colour as well as fabric. Anne's Sunday school teacher in L.M. Montgomery's *Anne of Green Gables* gets it right when she opens the door to her tea-time guest wearing:

> *The sweetest dress of pale pink organdie, with dozens of frills and elbow sleeves.*

Charlotte Brontë and Arnold Bennett on high tea

With sufficient additions, afternoon tea morphed into high tea: a substantial meal with an array of savoury foods accompanied by cakes, tarts and trifles, ideally homemade rather than the elaborate work of a confectioner. Typically, the savoury dishes of high tea are simpler than the main course of dinner: meat pies, or cold sliced meat or 'the dished-up piece of fish or toasted cheese' chosen by Lucia and her friends, rather than roasts or complex preparations with sauces.

Like afternoon tea, high tea differs from today's dinner in that all the food appears on the table together rather than in a sequence of courses. This all-at-once presentation derives from Eighteenth-Century dinners, when a course was many dishes arranged on the table so diners chose what they liked rather than eating of every one, just as they do at high tea. Indeed, one explanation of the phrase 'high tea' is that people sit up at a dining table whereas for afternoon tea – sometimes called 'low tea' – they snuggle into an armchair with a low table, perhaps set before the fire as in Barbara Pym's *Jane and Prudence*, when Jane's tea for church members includes Victoria sandwich, chocolate biscuits and small cakes bought from the local café-cum-bakery.

Charlotte Brontë pinpointed the difference between high tea and afternoon tea in *Shirley*, when the unexpected arrival of three curates at Caroline Helstone's Yorkshire home sends the maid scurrying out for 'some muffins and crumpets, and some biscuits' to buttress the usual tea-time supplies:

> *Yorkshire people in those days took their tea round the table. ... It was essential to have a multitude of plates of bread and butter, varied in sorts and plentiful in quantity: it was thought proper too that on the centre-plate should stand a glass dish of marmalade; among the viands were expected to be found a small assortment of cheesecakes and tarts; if there was also a plate of thin slices of pink ham garnished with green parsley, so much the better.*

The link to dinner is even clearer in Arnold Bennett's vigorous descriptions of Mrs. Sutton's high teas in *Anna of the Five Towns*. When Anna attends the Sewing Circle, she discovers:

> *The board was richly spread with fancy breads and cakes, jams of Mrs. Sutton's own celebrated preserving, diverse sandwiches compiled by Beatrice, and one or two large examples of the famous Bursley pork-pie.*

When Anna and Mynors get engaged, Mrs. Sutton lays on a veritable feast:

> *The tea, made especially magnificent in honour of the betrothal, was such a meal as could only have been compassed in Staffordshire or Yorkshire – a high tea of the last richness and excellence, exquisitely gracious to the palate, but ruthless in its demands on the stomach. At one end of the table, which glittered with silver, glass and Longshaw china, was a fowl which had been boiled for four hours; at the other, a hot pork-pie islanded in liquor, which*

might have satisfied a regiment. Between these two dishes were all the delicacies which differentiate high tea from tea, and on the quality of which the success of the meal really depends; hot pikelets, hot crumpets, hot toast, sardines with tomatoes, raisin-bread, currant-bread, seed-cake, lettuce, home-made marmalade, and home-made hams.

Who eats what, where and how

The Suttons manufacture china in Arnold's fictional version of his home town Stoke-on-Trent. Just as afternoon tea was adapted to aristocratic and metropolitan homes where dinner came late, high tea was suited to those who worked in offices and factories. They were still on the job when afternoon tea came at four o'clockish. By the time they got home, they were ready for a serious meal. High tea filled the bill with its array of dishes: some sweet, some savoury; some homemade, some bought from a bakery or pork butcher's.

While the Suttons' tea marks them as business people of the North and Midlands, enjoying wealth and ample fare, the simple tea of coconut cakes and fruit identify the poor but professional Hales in Mrs. Gaskell's *North and South*. Just so, the lavish supply of hotcakes followed by orange cake and chocolate cake consumed by Mrs. Vermont and the hunting teas so common in Molly Keane's novels mark the setting as Ireland. In *Shirley* Charlotte Brontë's Caroline Helstone shows a proper northern welcome to the curates, even though they are a bit of a nuisance, serving them a substantial high tea. Other hostesses are not so hospitable. When Agnes, the governess at the centre of Anne Brontë's *Agnes Grey* visits her former pupil Rosalie, now married, she is told:

Now you shall have some tea – it will soon be dinner time, but, I thought, as you were accustomed to dine at one, you

> *would perhaps like better to dine when we lunch; and then, as you know, you can have your tea in this room, and that will save you from having to dine with Lady Ashby and Sir Thomas.*

Eating tea alone is the social opposite of sitting around the well-furnished Yorkshire tea table evoked by Charlotte Brontë in *Shirley*. In effect, Agnes is being told that as a governess she is too lowly to share the late dinner of titled people. She must follow the workaday custom of dinner at midday, with tea later – the custom that prevailed at the Brontë home, Haworth Parsonage.

Beyond high tea and afternoon tea

The words 'high' and 'afternoon' are not the only way to characterise tea-time – nor necessarily the most revealing. When Anna returns from one of the Suttons' sumptuous teas, her little sister, whose miserly father provides only basic sustenance, asks 'Did they have cakes or was it a plain tea?' A plain tea would have had only bread and butter. In *Of Human Bondage* Philip and his friend decide on 'a stodgy tea', a satisfying feast of buns, muffins, crumpets and cake.

In contrast, a cream tea assures that cream will appear, either whipped or clotted, usually with scones and jam, or in the south-west in buns called splits. Similarly identifying the main food, Margaret Drabble in *The Sea Lady* describes a typical 1950s seaside boarding-house, whose tariff includes breakfast and a fish tea – probably fish and chips or boiled fish with parsley sauce. Mentioning a meat tea of the same era in *Jane and Prudence*, Barbara Pym neatly defines the difference between high tea and afternoon tea. When the parish ladies who have been sorting clothes for a jumble sale are summoned to the dining-room for tea, Jane wonders whether it is to be a meat tea – which would have perhaps had boiled ham or tongue – or fish and chips, but is quite happy with toast, sandwiches, and several sorts of cake.

Tea breakfasts, Christmas tea and other tea occasions

Other adjectives define the occasion for tea rather than its centrepiece treat, though the traditional food for the occasion is often implicit. For example, in 1750 William Ellis noted that in Cheshire, oat bread was everyday fare. On the rare occasions when people ate wheat bread, 'It is commonly of the very whitest sort, for making manchet to eat at a tea breakfast.'

For much of the Twentieth Century a child's birthday tea absolutely had to have jelly and blancmange, preferably made in a mould, and usually prefaced by simple sandwiches filled with egg and cress or meat paste and followed by fairy cakes or iced fancies and birthday cake. Christmas tea must have its snowy Christmas cake. In Dylan Thomas's *A Child's Christmas in Wales*, it comes after the assembled uncles have snored through post-Christmas dinner naps, and Auntie Hannah has sustained herself with several little drinks:

> *And then at tea the Uncles would be jolly and the iced cake loomed in the centre of the table like a marble grave. Auntie Hannah laced her tea with rum because it was only once a year.*

More temperately, you could be sure there was no alcohol at chapel anniversary teas: just giant metal pots of tea and plenty of sandwiches and pastel-iced cakes or buns. Just so at village fêtes: in Virginia Woolf's *Between the Acts* as gentry Mrs. Manresa and Mrs. Porter get their tea before the villagers:

'What delicious tea!' each exclaimed, disgusting though it was, like rust boiled in water. And the cake fly-blown. But they had a duty to society.

More enticingly, a hunting tea always comes with eggs. When the cook in Molly Keane's *Good Behaviour* takes off with the driver of the bakery van, the parlour maid rustles up tea rather than dinner, and carries it in, saying:

I brought ye a hunting tea. ... The eggs were perfect, swelling primly on large slices of buttered toast, the lightest dust of cayenne blown over their well-matched pearls.

Tango Teas

Tea can also be characterised by the events that take place around it. Office tea resonates of the days when a tea trolley with tea and biscuits came round the office. Much more splendid were the Tango Teas at the Savoy Hotel in London in the 1920s. Manager Sir George Reeves-Smith, a tango enthusiast, arranged for several dancing schools to teach the steps, and hired bands and dancers to perform. In this way he had good music, skilled dancers and a clientèle eager to show off their footwork. The slogan 'If you can walk, you can tango' encouraged the faint-hearted, and they came in droves to enjoy the dancing and a menu that featured ice-cream and chocolates, then, like cakes, familiar presences on afternoon tea menus.

Tango teas were a variant of *thé dansante* or tea dances where people could show their paces in the new foxtrot and Charleston. In the 1920s and 1930s, hotels put them on in all major cities. But the Second World War swept everyone into other activities, and when it was over, the fashion had faded. Now, the working day makes them impossible for most younger people, but they have migrated to church and community halls, where the elderly enjoy them in retirement.

Tea urns

In wealthy homes, the presence of servants making tea could dampen the conversation. This problem was solved in the late Eighteenth Century by the tea urn. William Taylor, a London footman, described a tea urn in his 1837 diary:

They have hot water come up in an urn that has a place in the middle for a red hot iron which keeps the water boiling as long as the iron keeps hot. With this they make their tea themselves.

Explaining English customs for their American audience, Harriet Beecher Stowe and her sister Catherine wrote in 1869:

The first article of faith is that the water must not be merely hot, not merely to have boiled a few moments since, but actually be boiling the moment it touches the tea. Hence, though servants in England are vastly better trained than with us, this delicate mystery is rarely left to their hands. Tea-making belongs in the drawing room and high-born ladies preside at the 'bubbling and loud-hissing urn', and see that all due rites and solemnities are properly performed – that all cups are hot, and that the infused tea waits the exact time before libations commence.

By the Twentieth Century however, the large urn was distracting. In Arnold Bennett's *Anna of the Five Towns* the Suttons' daughter, Beatrice, takes a reforming hand:

The ancient clumsy custom of having tea urns on the table itself had been abolished by Beatrice, who had read in a paper that carving was now never done at the table, but by a neatly dressed parlour-maid. Consequently the tea urns were exiled to the sideboard, and the tea dispensed by a couple of maids. Thus, as Beatrice had explained to her mother, the hostess was left free to devote herself to the social arts.

The best bone china

Just like the food served at tea, and regardless of whether the tea itself is an elegant infusion or a boring old bag, the china it is served in also indicates temperament and class.

This is especially the case for distressed gentlefolk because bone china is so much more durable than money. Impoverished ladies have been able to drink their tea from lovely cups long after the funds that bought them have gone the way of the world. Like Mrs. Gaskell's Cranford ladies, the Crowhurst twins in Molly Keane's *Good Behaviour* can scarcely rub two pennies together, yet drink 'China tea out of thin shallow cups', only switching to cheaper Indian tea as their money finally expires. In *Jane and Prudence* the fastidiousness that distinguishes Prudence is clear when she sits in solitary elegance sipping expensive Lapsang Souchong from a delicate white and gold cup. Similarly, the Countess Olenska in Edith Wharton's *Age of Innocence* has a more refined taste than other gilded-age New Yorkers, serving tea in 'handleless Japanese cups and little covered dishes' that reflect the late-Nineteenth-Century discovery of Japanese art.

But for the real intricacies of the teacup, May Sinclair is the most precise. When Mrs. Beauchamp entertains Canon

Chamberlain in *The Cure of Souls*, each sees, for the first time, how much they have in common:

It was delicious, sitting there in the deep, soft-cushioned chair, eating hot buttered scones, drinking China tea with the smoky flavour he loved, and watching the plump but dainty hands hovering about the teacups and dishes. Mrs. Beauchamp enjoyed tea-time and was determined that he should enjoy it too. The teacups – he noticed such things – were wide and shallow, and had a pattern of light green and gold on white, with a broad green and gold band inside, under the brim. His nostrils drank in the fragrance.

'I wonder why it is,' he said, 'that a green lining to a cup makes tea so much more delicious. But it does.'

'I know it does,' she said with feeling.

'There's a house where they give you strong Indian tea in dark-blue china. You can't imagine anything more horrible.'

'It would be.'

'And all teacups should be wide and shallow.'

'Yes, it's like champagne in wide glasses, isn't it?'

'A larger surface for the scent, I suppose.'

'Funny that there should be light green tastes and dark-blue tastes, but there are. Only I didn't think anybody noticed but me.'

Others, in fact, had noticed. In 1906, the Japanese tea historian, Okakura Kakuzo paraphrased Lu Yu on Chinese cups:

Lu Yu considered the blue as the ideal colour for the teacup, as it lent additional greenness to the beverage, whereas the white made it look pinkish and distasteful. It was because he used cake-tea. Later on when the tea-masters of Sung took to the powdered teas they preferred heavy bowls of blue-black and dark brown. The Mings with their steeped tea, rejoiced in lighter ware of white porcelain.

Silver teapots

China teapots were as popular as the teacups they matched, but though enviable, they lacked the shining prestige of silver teapots.

In the early days of tea in Britain, drinking from silver teacups was impossible because they are too hot to hold, but silver teapots were serviceable because, unlike earthenware, they did not crack when filled with boiling water. The first English silver teapot was presented to the Committee of the East India Company in 1670. Even after English potteries had learned the secret of making china that resisted the thermal shock of boiling water in the late Eighteenth Century, silver teapots retained their cachet. As a mark of respect to her guests, Caroline Helstone gets the silver set from the plate closet when the curates arrive for tea in *Shirley*. In Molly Keane's *Loving Without Tears* the housekeeper Birdie makes tea in a 'rosebud china teapot' for the kitchen staff while the footman Finn makes tea for the drawing room in 'a silver teapot and hot-water jug'. In Dorothy Sayers' *Busman's Honeymoon* Harriet notes the class implications of silver versus china when she pours tea for her new husband Lord Peter Wimsey. Her frosty new sister-in-law, the Duchess of Denver, would scorn Harriet's chipped china pot, insisting on aristocratic silver, even if the pot were empty. Presumably the Duchess would not have concerned herself about the opinion common among tea experts that tea actually tastes better out of earthenware or china, rather than from silver or other metal pots.

The triumph of tea

No one has written more feelingly about tea than Okakura Kakuzo. One of his aims was to explain Japanese culture to Isabella Stewart-Gardner and her late-Nineteenth-Century Boston circle. To make a connection between East and West he wrote:

Afternoon and Other Tea-times

The afternoon tea is now an important function in western society. In the delicate clatter of trays and saucers, in the soft rustle of feminine hospitality, in the common catechism about cream and sugar, we know that the Worship of tea is established beyond question.

In Britain, the myriad of sandwiches, the breads and cakes, the bright jams and fragrant teas, the pretty china and gleaming silver teapot combine to make tea-time the acme of relaxation, comfort, and triumph over stress. Muriel Spark captured this movingly in *Memento Mori*. When 86-year-old Charmian Piper makes her own tea she conquers age, forgetfulness and weakness. Left alone in the house, she fills the kettle – just half full because it's heavy – spoons tea in the pot, then adds water, and takes the teapot to the tray. Even though her hand is unsteady, she doesn't spill any. She fills the hot water jug, then realises that she cannot carry a tea tray loaded with both a teapot and hot water, so she takes them one at a time to the library, followed by trips to take scones and the Garibaldi biscuits she likes dipping into her tea. It takes her twenty minutes to get everything set up, and then she has to have a little nap before she can sip her tea. But the bliss of being alone and able to enjoy tea-time without the interference of the obnoxious Mrs. Pettigrew, who supposedly cares for her, makes it all worthwhile.

This enjoyment refracts from many literary mirrors. In *Bitter Lemons* Lawrence Durrell mocks it as his aged compatriots tottering to tea at the Dome Hotel in Kyrenia in the dreary post-war years to a flock of 'dejected waterfowls and crows'.

In Somerset Maugham's *Cakes and Ale* the narrator says he had heard Driffield, the writer who was the gorgeous Rosie's first husband, say that Henry James had neglected to write about the rise of the United States, his country of origin, in order to detail the tittle-tattle of tea parties in England, the country he adopted.

More typically, writers emphasise the sheer pleasure of tea. Thomas De Quincy wrote:

Surely everyone is aware of the divine pleasures which attend the wintry fireside: candles at four o'clock, warm hearthrugs, a fair tea-maker, shutters closed, curtains flowing in ample draperies to the floor, while the wind and rain are raging audibly without.

In his late-Nineteenth-Century novel *The Private Papers of Henry Ryecroft*, George Gissing concurred:

One of the shining moments of my day is that, when having returned a little weary from an afternoon walk, I exchange boots for slippers, out-of-doors coat for easy, familiar, shabby jacket and in my deep soft elbowed chair, await the tea tray... how delicious is the soft penetrating odour which floats into my study with the teapot!

In Barbara Pym's *Jane and Prudence* Jane believes that the angst of the characters in Ibsen's plays would be eased if one of them thought of making life easier by making a cup of tea.

The working day and tea times

Many share Jane's belief that tea can help in almost any situation – a conviction that goes back to the beginnings of tea in China. But as fewer women spend their days as housewives and servants are a rarity, the fully-fledged afternoon tea has disappeared from most homes, replaced, perhaps, by a cup of tea and a biscuit.

Afternoon tea or a cream tea with scones and jam and cream is now a treat in an hotel or tea room on a day out.

This has made it more luxurious. Three-tier stands come freighted with scones, cream, jam, miniature cakes, biscuits, and sandwiches with savoury fillings. Gone is plain bread and butter, once the essential prelude, and while the pot of tea is as important as ever, a truly sumptuous tea comes with champagne or a martini as well. By becoming an occasional treat rather than a regular daily event, afternoon tea has grown even more delightful.

High tea has changed much less. Always the meal of the middle class and working class, it retains its convenience as a quick substantial meal after the workday. Many people now call this meal 'supper'; for others, it's simply 'tea'. Whatever it's called, today's high teas are clearly a version of the hearty fare Arnold Bennett described in the Sutton home, with pizzas replacing crumpets and pikelets, and burgers beating out the meat pies, sliced ham and cold fowl that used to star in it.

CHAPTER 4

Love and Marriage at the Tea Table

Her two red lips affected Zephyrs blow,
To cool Bohea, and inflame the Beau,
While one white finger and a thumb conspire
To lift the cup and make the world admire.

Edward Young, *The Love of Fame, the Universal Passion*

THE PRIMROSE path of tea-table dalliance meanders through enticing landscapes, sometimes glimpsing the heights of passion but more often opening onto vistas of togetherness. As fictional lovers pause for tea, readers see the prospects that lure them on. Often, too, they spot the pitfalls hidden on the flowery path, and can guess who will blunder into its sloughs, and who will find the happy home that lies at its end.

Sugar-tong fingers

Tea for two – and only two – is the thought that seizes John Thornton when he visits the Hales in Mrs. Gaskell's *North and South.* Their simple tea of fruit and coconut cakes looks delightful, but Margaret Hale eclipses it:

She looked as if she were not attending to the conversation, but was solely busy with the tea cups, among which her round ivory hands moved with pretty, noiseless daintiness. She had a bracelet on one taper arm, which would fall down over her round wrist. Mr Thornton watched the re-placing of this troublesome ornament with far more attention than he listened to her father. It seemed as if it fascinated him to see her push it up impatiently, until it tightened her soft flesh. ... He almost longed to ask her to do for him what he saw her compelled to do for her father, who took her little finger and thumb in his masculine hand and made them serve as sugar tongs.

Inflaming the beau

Sugar-tong fingers seem a rare appetite, but men in Nineteenth-Century novels invariably melted at the sight of 'round ivory hands' like Margaret's. Rosamond Vincy, always keen to display her charms, is shown 'delicately handling the tea service with her taper fingers' in George Eliot's *Middlemarch*. Mrs. Beauchamp's 'plump but dainty hands hovering about the teacups' set Canon Chamberlain on the path to marriage in May Sinclair's *A Cure of Souls*.

Lily Bart's choices

Tea for two as a prelude to marriage is also on Lily Bart's mind as she serves tea to Percy Gryce in Edith Wharton's *House of Mirth*. They are travelling by train to a Long Island house party, and lovely Lily knows she must soon find a wealthy husband to keep her in the manner to which she has accustomed herself. Percy has pots of money and as he is already half in love with Lily, the third-rate railway tea only adds to her allure. Percy can't take his eyes off her hands:

They flitted above the tea tray looking miraculously fine and slender in contrast to coarse china and lumpy bread.

But for Lily the 'inky' tea drunk with Percy compares poorly to the Russian caravan tea she had earlier sipped with her friend Lawrence Selden – the only man who understands her dilemma. 'One of the charms of tea is the fact of drinking it together,' she thinks. Rich but tedious Percy is on the hook, but reeling him means wallowing with him at tea-time for the rest of her life. Tea with Selden is alluring, but financially he can't swing her into the golden realms of New York society. Should she nonetheless try to marry him?

Wharton's novel turns on questions about who Lily should or could marry. A clue lies in the tea-time roles she plays in these early scenes. Lily and Selden had made and enjoyed tea *tête à tête*, but in his home not hers. With Percy she is again rattling along to someone else's house. Lily has no place to call her own. And she has no settled opinion either. Undoubtedly, Percy is – and has – just what she claims to have hoped for in a husband, yet he does not satisfy her, and neither does Selden. Lily drifts from man to man, as she does from house to house. While Margaret Hale's bracelet and pincing fingers hint at bonds that will tie her and Thornton together, Lily's wanderings and hand-to-mouth stratagems suggest that, surprisingly, she is not really committed to marrying – and in her world that is fatal.

Nothing for Pip

In Charles Dickens' *Great Expectations* tea-time *à deux* also forecasts the outcome of marriage hopes. Miss Havisham has told Pip to give Estella tea in an hotel. He describes the occasion:

> *I rang for tea, and the waiter ... brought by degrees some fifty adjuncts to that refreshment, but of tea not a glimpse.*

A teaboard, cups and saucers, plates, knives and forks (including carvers), spoons (various), salt cellars, a meek little muffin confined with the utmost precaution under a strong iron cover, Moses in the bulrushes typified by a soft bit of butter in a quantity of parsley, a pale loaf with a powdered head, two proof impressions of the bars of the kitchen fire place on triangular bits of bread, and ultimately a fat family urn, which the waiter staggered in with, expressing in his countenance burden and suffering. After a prolonged absence at this stage of the entertainment he at length came back with a casket of precious appearance containing twigs. These I steeped in hot water, and so from the whole of these appliances I extracted one cup of I don't know what for Estella.

The hardness of that strong iron cover and the dryness of the bar-marked toast, the powdery loaf, the twiggy tea – all characterise the desert of Estella's heart. This comfortless occasion suggests that Pip is doomed to more serious disappointment than simply lack of a cup of tea.

Treats for the sweet

In contrast, a more generous supply of food augurs well. When the Reverend Balwhidder has his eye on Mrs. Nugent as his third wife in John Galt's *Annals of the Parish*, her invitation to tea is a signal that she is interested. Agreement is reached over a chicken:

Dr. Dinwhiddie put one wing on Mrs. Nugent's plate and the other wing on my plate and said there have been greater miracles than these two wings flying together, which was a sharp joke that caused no little merriment at the expense of Mrs. Nugent and me. I, however, to show I was none daunted, laid a leg also on her plate, and took another on my own, saying in the words of the Reverend Doctor, there have been greater miracles than that these two legs should lay in the same nest.

Similarly, in Molly Keane's Irish novels giving tea-time treats to someone you fancy is a good first move. In *Loving Without Tears* Birdie captures the attention of the man she has her eye on while he's sitting in her kitchen.

He looked back at Birdie, who was lightly filling her wafers of coarse-grained brown bread with a coral and cream mixture of lobster and a hint of jade and pearl in chopped lettuce. 'A wonderful cuisine,' he murmured. Birdie's eyes lifted again from her work. 'Will you have a new laid egg for your tea?' she invited. ... She put the plate of sandwiches down on the table in the window and carried the rosebud china teapot ... to a kettle on the range.

(Lobster and lettuce sandwich recipe, p. 154.) Tea-time eggs signal affection in all Keane's novels. In *Taking Chances* Mary, who is about to wreak havoc on several hearts, is wooed with eggs:

'Now Mary,' says Roguey, 'have some tea. Are you hungry? Are you hot? You'll be cold if you sit there. Now have an egg. Yes, you must have an egg. Of course you must!' Poached eggs, faintly orange and milky white; toast, butter, tea – thin scalding China tea; red jelly in a white pot.

Anthony Trollope approached the matter more indirectly. Early in *Rachel Ray* he describes the comfortable teas Rachel and her mother enjoy while Dorothea, the high-thinking older sister, is off sacrificing herself:

At five o'clock Rachel would slip away and make hot toast, and would run over the Green to Farmer Sturt's wife for a little thick cream, and there would be a batter cake and so there would be a feast. Rachel was excellent at such banquets, knowing how to coax the teapot into a good drawing humour, and being very clever in little comforts.

Later, when Luke Rowan comes to tea intending to ask Mrs. Ray to accept him as Rachel's suitor, the scene is repeated as Rachel runs off again for cream:

'I hope you like clotted cream,' said Rachel taking off her hat. Luke declared that it was the one thing in all the world that he liked best, and that he had come to Devonshire with the express object of feasting upon it for the rest of his life.

This near repetition of the first scene shows Rachel's domesticity and love extending to Luke, and his enthusiasm for Devonshire and its clotted cream reverberate later when Rachel fears he may not return. After tea Luke and Mrs. Ray chat while Rachel thinks, 'But what could be nicer than this – to sit and listen to him in her mother's presence?'

The scene shows that Luke and Rachel suit each other perfectly. The opposition of Luke's mother and the dithering of Mrs. Ray notwithstanding, readers realise they will indeed marry, and live in Devonshire with all the clotted cream they could ever want. (Recipe for batter cake, pp. 146–7.)

Rivals at tea

If giving favourite delicacies charms a beloved, then giving them to someone else shows when hope is vain. In 1711, Laurence Eusden wrote in *The Spectator*:

I saw a gentleman turn as pale as ashes because an idol turned the sugar in a tea-dish for his rival.

Rivals battle over tea as Gwendolen and Cecily do when tea-time confidences suggest they are both engaged to the same man in Oscar Wilde's *The Importance of Being Earnest*. Cecily asks Gwendolen if she takes sugar. Gwendolen declines, saying: 'Sugar is not fashionable any more.' Cecily drops four lumps into her cup. 'Cake or bread and butter?' she asks. Gwendolen replies:

> *Bread and butter, please. Cake is rarely seen in the best houses now-a-days.*

So, of course, Cecily cuts her 'a very large slice of cake'. Gwendolen warns: 'You may go too far', but Cecily is defiant:

> *To save my poor, innocent, trusting boy from the machinations of any other girl there are no lengths to which I would not go.*

Similarly, in Barbara Pym's *Jane and Prudence* Jessie and Prudence both hope that Fabian will propose. When he invites them to tea, Jessie worries that he will ask Prudence to pour tea for his guests, which would imply he planned to marry her. Fortunately, Fabian sees that asking either woman will discombobulate the other, so he gets his housekeeper to do the job. The Vicar cheerfully thinks this will obviate any hard feelings. But, Jessie spills tea on Prudence's dress, so hard feelings ensue, though the mishap – if that is what it really was – suggests who will win Fabian in the end.

Spilt tea spells conflict also in Emily Brontë's *Wuthering Heights*. When, after a three-year absence, Heathcliff calls on Catherine, now married to Edgar Linton, she is so elated that she invites him into the parlour so he and Edgar can become friends. To Edgar, Heathcliff is no more than a servant, to be entertained, if at all, in the kitchen, but he accedes:

> *'Sit down sir,' he said at length. 'Mrs. Linton, recalling old times, would have me give you a cordial reception, and, of course, I am gratified when anything occurs to please her.'*

Not the warmest of welcomes! Heathcliff counters that he, too, is gratified when things please Catherine. 'Especially if it be anything in which I have a part.' Soon 'pale with pure annoyance' at Catherine and Heathcliff's delight in each other, Edgar hastens them to the tea table, noting that Heathcliff faces a long walk afterwards – a strong hint that he will not be invited to stay overnight. These animosities play havoc with tea-time. Though Catherine takes her 'post before the urn', the servant Nelly notes:

> *The meal hardly endured ten minutes – Catherine's cup was never filled, she could neither eat nor drink. Edgar made a slop in his saucer, and scarcely swallowed a mouthful. Their guest did not protract his stay.*

Command of the tea table

Catherine's 'post before the urn' was her right as a married woman. Though she is little swayed by such traditions, command of the tea table was a position of power, and traditionally married women had the unquestioned right to wield it. Millamant had made this clear when she demanded 'To be sole Empress of my Tea-table' before agreeing to marry Mirabell in Congreve's *The Way of the World*.

In *The Tenant of Wildfell Hall* by Anne Brontë, Helen Huntingdon shares Millamant's conviction that having charge of the tea table equates to being married. When she realises her husband's infidelity, she immediately refuses to make tea for him or serve it to his guests; in effect, she will no longer live as his wife: 'I am your child's mother and your housekeeper – nothing more.'

Helen's position is extreme, and Anne Brontë's portrayal of the unfairness of the marriage laws of the 1840s shocked patriarchal Victorians. But the tradition that a wife reigned at the tea table survived, though often more happily. Harriett Vane affirms her new status as Lord Peter Wimsey's wife in Dorothy Sayers' *Busman's Honeymoon* when she points out to him that her presence, pouring his tea out of a pot with a chipped spout is evidence of their newly married state. Similarly, when Paul Morel brings Clara to tea in D.H. Lawrence's *Sons and Lovers* the attractive tea table exemplifies the dignity his mother has preserved despite a difficult marriage:

> *At tea Clara felt the refinement and sang-froid of the household. Mrs. Morel was perfectly at her ease. The pouring out of the tea and attending to the people went on unconsciously, without interrupting her talk. ... The china of dark blue willow pattern looked pretty on the glossy cloth. There was a little bowl of small yellow chrysanthemums.*

The willow pattern story

Romance can easily take wing over a delicate cup of tea with elegant morsels of food, and never more operatically so than in the two birds fluttering eternally above the fray on willow pattern china.

When they lived in human form, these birds were called Koon-tse and Chang. She was the daughter of a wealthy mandarin who lived in the house in the centre of the plate, and Chang was but a poor secretary. When they fell in love, her angry father betrothed Koon-tse to a horrid old man, expelled Chang, and built a palisade to keep the lovers apart. But while the old man was drinking his head off at the betrothal, Chang arrived disguised as a beggar, and fled with Koon-tse and her betrothal jewels. We see them running across the bridge: Koon-tse with the distaff of virginity, Chang with the jewel box, and the furious father with a whip. Chang had arranged for a boat, and he and Koon-tse headed upstream to the island in the upper left of the plate. There they lived happily, cultivating their bit of land until the old man discovered them and had Chang slain as he tried to escape over the bridge. In desperation, Koon-tse burned their house. She died in the blaze, but the gods took pity and transformed the lovers into birds: emblems of constancy presiding over the mortal scene below.

Tea-time match-making

Married women took pride in being empress of their tea tables, but mothers alert to the charms of pretty hands pouring tea and eyelids batting over the cups sometimes asked marriageable daughters to preside. Thus, in *North and South* Margaret Hale captivates John Thornton when she serves tea in her mother's place.

This privilege could be whisked away when a daughter did not fall in with her parents' wishes. When Clarissa Harlowe rejects Soames's proposal in Samuel Richardson's *Clarissa*, she goes down to tea only to find an icy atmosphere:

> *My mother's eyes were fixed upon the tea cups and when she looked up it was heavily, as if her eyelids had weights on them, and then not at me.*

Clarissa asks if she should make tea, as normal:

> *No! A very short sentence, in one very short word, was the expressive answer. And she was pleased to take the canister in her own hands.*

Tea-time and proposals: the case of Emma

Emma Woodhouse in Jane Austen's *Emma* rules the tea table because her mother is dead. She shows how well she does the job early in the novel when she makes sure that Mr. Woodhouse doesn't unwittingly deprive Miss Bates and other guests of choice dishes by excessive concern for their health. At the end of the novel she returns to the tea table after Mr. Knightly has proposed. She had been walking in the shrubbery after dinner, remorseful at the muddle she has made by meddling. Mr. Knightly is equally unhappy because he believes she loves Frank Churchill. When he realises his mistake, he asks her to marry him. Her acceptance changes life for both of them:

> *The one half hour had given each the same precious certainty of being beloved, and had cleared from each the same degree of ignorance, jealousy, or distrust. ... They sat down to tea – the same party round the same table – But never in such a state of spirits, never in anything like it; and it was with difficulty that she could summon enough of her usual self to be the attentive lady of the house.*

The lack of detail in this proposal, the emphasis on transformation conjured by 'never in such a state of spirits, never in anything like it', lets the reader's imagination paint Emma's delight and floods the scene with meaning.

Notably, Mr. Knightly does not actually propose at the tea table. Nor do other fictional lovers. As a gathering place for a family and guests, the tea table is too public for intimate requests. But it's a perfect setting for all the moments that lead up to a proposal. John Thornton falls in love with Margaret Hale; Rachel Ray realises that life would be perfect with Luke Rowan and Percy Gryce loses himself to Lily Bart. The tea table can be an arena where rivals like Cecily and Gwendolen tussle for the men they want, or a sanctuary where lovers tempt each other with delicious morsels. Then, after the flirtations and first steps, innuendoes and intuitions of love, the tea table sets the scene for the married affection evoked by George Eliot in *Middlemarch*:

> *Mrs. Vincy herself sat at the tea-table. She resigned no domestic function to her daughter; and the matron's blooming good-natured face, with the too volatile pink strings floating round her throat and her cheery manners to her husband and children were certainly among the great attractions of the Vincy house – attractions which made it all the easier to fall in love with the daughter.*

Chapter 5

Children at Tea

I believe I could be a model child if I were just invited out to tea every day!

L.M. Montgomery, *Anne of Green Gables*

Validating Jane Eyre

Of all the poignant scenes in Charlotte Brontë's *Jane Eyre* none shines more brightly in the memory or comes as more of a relief to anxious readers than the tea-time Jane and Helen Burns spend with their headmistress, Miss Temple.

Jane's life has been filled with pain and humiliation, first as the unwelcome orphan in her aunt's house, and then, scorned, punished, and half-starved, as a pupil at Lowood – one of the most dreadful schools in all Victorian fiction. Even being invited into a room with a fire is luxury for Jane and Helen, but the warmth in Miss Temple's room is of the heart as well as of the hearth, and Jane comes away knowing that her virtues have been recognised – a vital sign that her life will improve.

The scene unfolds with a reminder of the harshness at the bitter core of Lowood:

> *How fragrant was the steam of the beverage, and the scent of the toast! Of which, however, I, to my dismay (for I was beginning to be hungry), discerned only a very small portion: Miss Temple discerned it too.*
>
> *'Barbara,' said she, 'can you not bring a little more bread and butter? There is not enough for three.'*

> *Barbara went out; she returned soon: – 'Madam, Mrs Harden says she has sent up the usual quantity.'*
> *Mrs. Harden, be it observed, was the housekeeper ... made up of equal parts whalebone and iron.*

Fortunately for Jane and Helen, Miss Temple has a 'good-sized seed-cake' (see recipe pp. 147–8) stashed in a drawer, and after giving the girls 'a cup of tea with one delicious but thin morsel of toast', she cuts generous slices. Jane and Helen, famished by burnt porridge and scant fare, are in heaven:

> *We feasted that evening as on nectar and ambrosia; and not the least delight of the entertainment was the smile of gratification with which our hostess regarded us, as we satisfied our famished appetites on the delicate fare she liberally supplied.*

This tea-time turns Jane's life in a new direction. Miss Temple tells her how she can disprove the accusation of being a liar. Later Jane does well at Lowood and gets a job as a governess at Thornfield Hall. When she arrives there after a long, cold drive, we see a parallel scene to tea with Miss Temple. Mrs. Fairfax settles her in a chair by the fire, and sends the servant for sandwiches. 'She treats me like a visitor!' Jane exults. Again, though the warm fire and comforting food and drink are more than welcome, Jane's joy is in being accepted as a person of account. She has been validated.

Coming-of-age

This pattern often repeats when fictional children are given tea. In *Harry Potter and the Sorcerer's Stone* by J.K. Rowling Harry is as persecuted as the young Jane Eyre: his uncle bullies him; his aunt nags him; his cousin pinches him; he is often hungry and frequently relegated to the spidery cupboard under the stairs. His deliverance will be going to Hogwarts School, but he knows nothing of this because his uncle throws away the acceptance letters. Yet for each one thrown away, more arrive. To avoid this postal cascade, his aunt and uncle take him to a remote hut. All of a sudden, the giant Hagrid appears. 'Couldn't make us a cup o'tea, could yeh?' he asks. Conjuring a fire in the cold grate, he takes a chocolate birthday cake from one massive pocket. A kettle, a teapot and mugs emerge next, followed by a poker and some squashy sausages to cook on it. When the sausages are done – actually slightly but deliciously burned – 'He passed the sausages to Harry, who was so hungry he had never tasted anything so wonderful, but still he couldn't take his eyes off the giant'. Soon he learns about his birthright as a wizard and the place reserved for him at Hogwarts. Harry's tea by the fire with Hagrid parallels Jane's tea by the fire with Miss Temple: it signals that he will not always be oppressed; his merits will find acknowledgement.

Less dramatically, when Mary persuades Colin to have tea in Frances Hodgson Burnett's *The Secret Garden*, the sick boy, who eats little and is never pleased with anything, also passes a milestone. Though he revives only slightly, his appreciative exclamation 'These muffins look so nice and hot!' shows that he can be warmed into life.

In effect, for Colin, Harry and Jane tea-times mark a turning point, even a coming-of-age, as they begin to move from difficult childhoods toward happier lives. (Recipe for muffins, pp. 131–2.)

Grown-uppish teas with Anne

The tale of *Anne of Green Gables* by L.M. Montgomery is entirely devoted to Anne's growing up in a world far more hospitable than the orphanage she lived in until the kindly Marilla and Matthew adopted her. She has to learn to channel her imagination and energies into the friendly but strait-laced ways of Avonlea. When Marilla goes out, telling her she can invite her friend Diana to tea, she exclaims 'It will be so nice and grown-uppish.' She begs to use the best rosebud spray tea-set, and knowing proper tea-time form, asks, 'Can I take her into the spare room to lay off her hat when she comes?' Marilla refuses this adult privilege, but provides plenty of other grown-uppish delights:

> *'No, indeed! The rosebud tea-set! You know I never use that except for the minister or the Aids. You'll put down the old brown tea-set. But you can use the little yellow crock of cherry preserves. It's time it was being used anyway – I believe it's beginning to work. And you can cut some fruitcake and have some of the cookies and snaps.'*
>
> *'I can just imagine myself sitting down at the head of the table and pouring out the tea,' said Anne, shutting her eyes ecstatically. 'And asking Diana if she takes sugar! I know she doesn't but of course I'll ask her just as if I didn't know. And pressing her to take another piece of fruitcake and another helping of preserves.'*

(Recipe for snaps, pp. 141–2.) Anne's visions of tea-time delights know few bounds. She's especially pleased when Marilla tells her:

> *There's a bottle half full of raspberry cordial left over from the church social the other night. It's on the second shelf of the sitting-room closet and you and Diana can have it if you like, and a cooky to eat with it along in the afternoon.*

The raspberry cordial will be Anne's Nemesis, but not before she and Diana, both dressed in their second best, shake hands and inquire after each other's family in correct lady-like style. When the time comes for the raspberry cordial, Anne finds it not on the second shelf, but on the top one. And Diana finds it delicious. 'That's awfully nice raspberry cordial Anne,' she says. Being the perfect little hostess, Anne replies:

> *'I am so glad you like it. Take as much as you want. I am going to run out and stir the fire up. There are so many responsibilities on a person's mind when they're keeping house, aren't there?'*

Three full tumblers later, Diana is feeling sick and totters away unsteadily, unable to eat anything. Next day it is revealed that unbeknownst to Anne the raspberry cordial was actually currant wine – definitely not approved by the church ladies of the temperance society, including Diana's mother.

Unlike many of the scrapes she gets into, this one is not Anne's fault. Still, the failed tea-party shows she's not yet entirely ready for the world. She does much better later when she goes to tea at her Sunday school teacher's house. She reports:

> *'We had an elegant tea, and I think I kept all the rules of etiquette pretty well.'*

Indeed, tea-time is her proving ground. Enthusing about its joys, she tells Marilla:

> *'I believe I could be a model child if I were just invited out to tea every day! ... Would it be good manners to take a second helping of anything if you wanted it very much?'*

Becoming human

Like Anne, the animals in Alison Uttley's *Little Grey Rabbit's Party* enjoy learning party rules. Hare watches a children's birthday party through a window. Squirrel and Little Grey Rabbit arrive in time to see them playing Hunt the Thimble

Sunday school teas and other children's treats

While affluent children of the Nineteenth and early Twentieth Centuries had tea in the nursery with a nanny who trained them in tea-time rules, working-class children had only occasional tea parties – usually special events laid on by Sunday schools or their parents' employers. In Arnold Bennett's *Anna of the Five Towns* the children go to the country for their annual Sunday school treat. After games they get a paper bag with 'bread and butter, currant cake, an Eccles cake and a Bath bun' (see recipes pp. 142–3 and 135–6). The cleaners and their children in Dorothy L. Sayers' *Murder Must Advertise* are hosted to a Charwomen's Tea. There's a bran tub for the children and new hair ribbons. In *Lark Rise to Candleford* Flora Thompson recalled a two-day annual village Feast. Sunday was a harvest home dinner, but the Monday 'was a great day for tea parties'. They were women-and-children-only events highlighted by 'baker's cake'. The mothers made the dough and added dried fruit in honour of the day; the village baker baked everyone's cake in his big oven, hence the name.

and Blind Man's Buff. Determined to have a party of their own, they get a book on party games from Wise Old Owl, and Little Grey Rabbit gets to work:

> *The preparations began. Grey Rabbit went shopping and came back with caraway seeds, candied peel, beechnut flour and cinnamon sticks. Squirrel looked in the woods and found hoards of nuts which she ground in a bowl. Hare brought a*

basket of eggs from Speckledy Hen. Every morning Hare learned his forfeits as though they were lessons. 'Cry in one corner, laugh in another, sing in another and dance in another,' he repeated.

Holly and mistletoe give this party a Christmassy feel, while the food is traditional children's party fare with some nutty treats to adapt it to the woodland animals:

There were pink cakes and white cakes, mince pies and hazelnut sandwiches and roasted chestnuts. In the middle was the party cake, covered with icing, which Hare had brought from the top of the pond.

(Recipe for hazelnut sandwiches, pp. 155–6.) They play the games they had learned, Grey Rabbit handing over her precious thimble as essential equipment for Hunt the Thimble. Unfortunately, Wise Old Owl, who has not bothered to master any of the ins and outs of tea parties, swallows it. The story ends with everyone gratified by their party, though Grey Rabbit is saddened by the loss of the thimble. Like Anne, they have proved pretty good at party protocol, but not perfect.

Revolutionary tea-times

Of course, protocol gets oppressive. Even though the charm of tea has always been closely linked to its casual comfort, etiquette books of the Nineteenth and early Twentieth Centuries pontificated on the dos and don'ts: Nannies trained children in the proper manners at nursery tea so eventually they could join their parents for afternoon tea. One strict rule was to eat bread and butter first, leaving cakes and fruit for later. Naturally that tormented tiny appetites since bread and butter could fill so much space that there was little room for the prettier and sweeter things.

In her cookery book *Nursery Cooking* novelist Molly Keane recalls an 'enlightened hostess' who cheered children doing their best to behave with the liberating cry 'Now! Let's start with the strawberries and cream.' A more melancholy memory of Molly Keane's is her Nanny refusing to let her eat sponge cake at a tea party, so she had to stick to bread and butter while other children made hay with sardine sandwiches and chocolate biscuits.

What a nasty Nanny!

Nobody was ever a better Nanny than P.L. Travers' Mary Poppins. She always knows when to turn the rules upside down. She makes her usual token protests but no real demur when her Uncle Albert laughs so much at his birthday party the room fills with laughing gas, and everyone becomes airborne. The tea-table with 'crumpets, coconut cakes and a large plum cake with pink icing' magically rises to join them somewhere near the ceiling. (Recipe for coconut cakes, pp. 138–9.) Uncle Albert says:

'It is usual I think to begin with bread and butter. ... But as it's my birthday we will begin the wrong way – which I always think is the "right" way – with the Cake!' And he cut a large slice for everyone.

Going home on the bus Mary Poppins denies they were ever in the air. Were they or were they not? It doesn't matter; in this book desire and imagination wait on reality. Mary's earlier tea-time with the Match Man had been just such an occasion. He has no money to take her to tea and eat the raspberry jam cakes she adores, so they step onto a picture he has drawn on the pavement, and soon find themselves strolling through a wood and into a sunlit glade, where there's a table set for afternoon tea:

A pile of raspberry jam cakes as high as Mary Poppins' waist stood in the centre, and beside it tea was boiling in a big brass urn. Best of all, there were two plates of whelks and two pins to pick them out with.

A waiter appears from behind a tree to serve them and Mary whispers to the Match Man 'We're having them after all.' (Recipe for raspberry jam cakes, pp. 140–1.) The scene ends with Mary and the Match Man back in the real world smiling because 'they knew ... what lay behind the trees' – a revolutionary world in which burdens like having no money and no raspberry jam cakes lighten as imagination shoulders the burden and makes life fun.

Topsy-turvy teas: mouse and bacon pie or veal and ham?

When imagination or magic or the edicts of the likes of Uncle Albert waltz away with tea-time rules, tea is generally funny as well as fun, and the fun easily twirls into farce.

In *The Pie and the Patty-Pan* Beatrix Potter turns the people and bedrooms of farcical tradition into pies and ovens.

The cat Ribby invites the dog Duchess to tea promising her 'something so very nice' baked in 'a pie dish with a pink rim'. Ribby tells Duchess she can eat the whole of this nice something because she herself will suffice with muffins. But Duchess had been planning to invite Ribby to tea, and has herself already made 'something most delicious' – a veal and ham pie, (recipe pp. 158–9). All she needs to do is pop it in the oven to bake. She worries that Ribby's menu will feature mouse, which she hates. But she knows the tea-party rules:

I really couldn't, couldn't *eat mouse pie. And I shall have to eat it because it's a party. And my pie was going to be veal and ham. A pink and white pie dish! And so is mine, just like Ribby's dish; they were both bought at Tabitha Twitchit's.*

What is a poor clever little dog to do? Knowing that Ribby will have to go out to buy muffins and will never taste the pie, Duchess decides to swap her veal and ham pie for Ribby's pie, which is indeed 'a pie of the most tender and delicate mouse minced up with bacon'.

Things work well at first. Ribby puts her pie in the bottom oven and goes for the muffins: Duchess dashes in; puts her pie in the top oven and runs back home to brush her hair. She returns at the proper time bearing flowers. Then, while Duchess is retrieving a sugar lump from under the table, Ribby takes the mouse and bacon pie from the oven. It 'proved extremely toothsome', and Duchess, believing it to be the veal and ham pie, wolfs down four pieces. Then disaster! Spooning out a fifth helping she realises she can't find the patty-pan she had put in to hold up the crust. She must have eaten it! Ribby assures her there is no patty-pan:

> *'I didn't put one in, my dear Duchess,' said Ribby. 'I don't think it necessary in pies made of mouse.'*

Only after Ribby has gone for a doctor, does the sizzling of the veal and ham pie in the top oven alert Duchess that there are two ovens and therefore two pies, and thus she has therefore certainly eaten mouse, and just as certainly not eaten a patty-pan. Now the business of hiding the veal and ham pie from Ribby spirals into another round of farce as she sticks it outside the back door, where the birds eat it, leaving only the patty-pan for Ribby to find next day.

This train of troubles would not have surprised Tabitha Twitchit. She had always disapproved of a party involving a cat and a dog, and she had her doubts about Ribby's menu too: 'A "pie" for afternoon tea! The very idea!' she said. Indeed, it is true: while baked foods such as scones, cakes, pastries, breads and even tarts are iconic afternoon tea fare, meat pies are more the stuff of high teas.

Tea rhymes

Farce, comedy and just plain ridiculousness also infuse lots of children's rhymes and skipping songs. One of the best-known is

Polly put the kettle on!
Polly put the kettle on!
Polly put the kettle on!
We'll all have tea.

Sukey take it off again!
Sukey take it off again!
Sukey take it off again!
We've all gone away.

The disappearance suggests teasing and hide-and-seek. Hiding also comes into the skipping song:

One, two, three
Mother caught a flea
Put it in the teapot to make a cup of tea
The flea jumped out
Mother gave a shout
Went around the corner
And bought a pint of stout.

The last two lines hark back to the centuries-old rivalry between tea and beer, suggesting that in such a teapot extremity, stout would be a steadying drink.

Such subversive rhymes make adults look more than usually silly. Other rhymes seem to be little more than nonsense, though they conjure up an appealing picture:

One day a pig went out to dig
For buttered buns for tea
He took a spade and a pick
And dug beside a tree.

Tea for school children

By the early Twentieth Century tea was so universally popular and cheap that children had long been drinking it. But knowledge about nutrition had improved, and doctors, dentists and social workers often deplored the diet of bread and tea that many children survived on. In *Rearing an Imperial Race*, a report of a 1913 Guildhall School conference on diet and hygiene in schools, several experts deplored tea. Speaking of the Scottish Highlands, a Dr. Murray reported:

> *The great feature in the decadence of the school child's mind is the abuse of tea. The good old porridge-pot has fallen from its high estate and the teapot is exalted in its place.*

The School Board of Glasgow came out firmly against giving tea to children under 14, while the Medical Officer for East Sussex advised:

> *Tea may consist of bread and butter, toast, buttered or plain, accompanied by jam or marmalade. If dinner has been small, something may be added as an egg or piece of bacon. The liquid should be cocoa rather than tea. I am firmly under the impression that tea should not be given to children under nine or ten.*

The Mad Hatter's tea party

A pig digging for buns, (recipe p. 135) has a Lewis Carroll air about him. Certainly Carroll created the most famous tea party in literature: the Mad Hatter's tea party in *Alice in Wonderland*. This tea party seems liberating because it breaks all of the rules, but its topsy-turviness becomes too much of a good thing.

The guests cluster at one end of a table laid for many more, yet they yell 'No room! No room!' when Alice approaches. The Dormouse tells a riddle, to which he doesn't know the answer. The Hatter has a watch that doesn't tell time. The Dormouse is dragooned into telling a story, but no-one listens. Alice gets no tea:

> *'Take some more tea,' the March Hare said to Alice, very earnestly.*
>
> *'I've had nothing yet,' replied Alice in an offended tone, 'so I can't take more.'*
>
> *'You mean you can't take "less",' said the Hatter: 'it's very easy to take more than nothing.'*
>
> *'Nobody asked* your *opinion,' said Alice.*

Surely this rude remark would have delighted Alice Liddell, the 10-year-old daughter of the Dean of Christ Church, Oxford, for whom Carroll wrote his tale: it was not at all the sort of thing expected of well-brought-up little girls in Victorian England.

Similarly, children delight in ridiculousness, especially when it involves not knowing the rules of life or doing things incorrectly. It is always tea-time in the Mad Hatter's ménage because his watch is fixed at 6 o'clock. The problem is that the March Hare had put butter in it. But the Hatter doesn't entirely blame the butter:

> *'Some crumbs must have got in as well,' the Hatter grumbled, 'you shouldn't have put it in with the bread-knife.' The March Hare took the watch and looked at it gloomily: then he dipped it into his cup of tea, and looked at it again: he could think of nothing better to say than his first remark, 'It was the "best" butter you know.'*

Compared to an everyday tea demanding best manners, tidy eating, and no putting things in the teapot, this scene is full of the no-nos and non sequiturs that thrill the under-10s.

Yet while children delight in spotting silliness and in overturning the rules when that means having cake or strawberries before boring old bread and butter, complete topsy-turviness alarms them. Alice tries hard to follow the scatty trail of the conversation at the Mad Hatter's table, but departs in disgust at his rudeness when she begins a sentence 'I don't think' and he jumps in with 'Then you shouldn't talk'. As she walks off, she looks back 'half hoping that they would call after her'.

They don't. The farcical mishaps of this tea party do not resolve at a second tea party like they do in *Anne of Green Gables*, nor are its mysteries clarified as in *The Pie and the Patty-Pan*. No-one recognises Alice's worth as Miss Temple does when she invites Jane Eyre to tea. Unlike Hagrid, who springs Harry from the prison of life with the Dursleys, the Mad Hatter is certainly not going to help Alice. He and the March Hare and the Dormouse could not care less when she wanders off into the wilderness of Wonderland.

Yet in its own bizarre way, the Mad Hatter's tea party validates Alice as other fictional tea parties assure children of their worth. It shows that she has kept her sense of self despite falling down the rabbit hole, consuming shape-shifting comestibles and weeping a sea of tears. The real madness of the tea party, and perhaps the reason it sticks so well in everyone's mind, is that it disobeys all the norms of language. The Hatter, the Hare and the Dormouse quibble endlessly about the meanings of words so they are eternally stuck in their mad world. Alice has the common sense to walk away from it, so it's clear she won't succumb to the craziness or end up like the Dormouse – stuffed into the teapot. She will survive – as will Jane, Harry, Colin, Anne and other children who share storybook tea-times.

CHAPTER 6

Tea Rooms

Tea! ... thou female tongue-running, smile-soothing, heart-opening ... cordial.

Colley Cibber

ABC of tea-room chains

Exhausted after a day of saving Britain from the threat of vampires, the hero of Bram Stoker's 1897 novel, *Dracula*, Jonathan Harker, writes:

I was tired and hungry. I got a cup of tea at the Aerated Bread Company and came down to Purfleet by the next train.

The Aerated Bread Company, better known as the ABC, had opened its first tea room at London Bridge in 1864. By the time *Dracula* appeared in 1897, its branches offered Londoners the relief that only a cup of tea can provide after a tiring day dicing with the dark forces of the world.

Tea at the ABC was cheap and service fast, so workers could get a quick lunch or cup of tea with toast or a bun to set them up for the rest of the day. It was a winning concept, and rival tea-room chains soon played their own variations on the theme.

The most famous was J. Lyons, which opened its first branches in the 1890s. By 1898 there were sixteen of them, and by the 1930s Lyons had 250 tea rooms as well as three Corner House restaurants each seating 3,000 people. Bigger branches were lavishly decorated with marble, gilt, and chandeliers. Musicians played while the waitresses, called Nippies, nipped around with laden trays. Their uniforms and lace-trimmed caps mimicked those of parlour maids; liveried doormen at larger branches looked like butlers, so customers could feel that they were enjoying the luxuries of wealth.

Its luxuries notwithstanding, Lyons kept prices low. In the 1890s it cost 2d for a pot of tea; elsewhere it was 3d a cup. Food prices were equally attractive: buns cost a penny, ice creams 3d, and cream meringues 5d. Hot meals were equally affordable with the most popular meal, roast beef and two vegetables, costing only tenpence.

Tea-room encounters

J.B. Priestley described the pleasures of Lyons in *Angel Pavement*, when Turgis goes to a 'giant teashop' on Saturdays. Like popular bars nowadays, it was the haunt of young people like himself, all hoping to meet someone. Turgis would love to hook up with one of the chattering lipsticked girls all hastening for their evening out. But even if he has no luck he's ready to enjoy the best tea of the whole fortnight – fish and chips, bread and butter and pastries – eaten beneath the twinkle of the chandeliers to the seductive music of the string orchestra. Smoking his cigarette at the end of his slap-up tea, Turgis feels soothed and contented.

Meeting someone new in a tea room was a real possibility. When novelist Barbara Pym was a WREN officer on leave in 1943 she recorded a chance tea-room encounter in her diary. It happened at a Lyons, where she sat with three soldiers, none of whom she knew, and talked about music. She described the occasion as a jolly tea, but noted that though many people enjoyed tea rooms because they brought people together in this way, she herself had previously found that the crowds and glittering décor made them lonely places. She was in a minority: opportunities for meeting the opposite sex were valued at an era when young people were still primly supervised, and privacy was often hard to come by. John Betjeman's poem *In a Bath Tea Shop* celebrates a tea-room rendezvous:

'Let us not speak for the love we bear one another –
Let us hold hands and look.'
She, such a very ordinary little woman;
He, such a thumping crook;
But both, for a moment, little lower than the angels
In the teashop's ingle nook.

Women and tea rooms

But while tea rooms could be a haven for both couples and tired workers, women have been their most devoted customers. In the Nineteenth Century, they needed refreshment when they were away from home. Men dominated both pubs, which were often riotous, and restaurants, which were not considered respectable for unchaperoned ladies until well into the Twentieth Century. The new tea rooms were a boon, and thus women enjoying cream buns (recipe pp. 135–6), such as those spotted by J.B. Priestley's Turgis could be seen in any branch of Lyons, or rivals such as Kardomah and Express Dairies.

Of these, none appealed to women more than Fuller's. Founded in Kensington in 1892, Fuller's tea rooms were smaller than Lyons. Friends met in cosy alcoves; tea came in elegant cups with beribboned tongs for the sugar and alluring pastries and cakes. Walnut cake was the most renowned (see recipe pp. 152–3), and memories of it still survive, though Fuller's tea rooms are no more. The cake was moist and crumbly, with thick white icing and halved walnuts conveniently placed so that each piece had its own nut. Just such a cake helped Charles Ryder demonstrate his mastery of the Oxford scene to his cousin Jasper in Evelyn Waugh's *Brideshead Revisited*. Determined to avoid any repetition of Jasper's intrusive advice about how to master the finer points of Oxford manners, he serves him a tea to impress, with Fuller's walnut cake adding glory to the honey buns and anchovy toast that preceded it.

The economics of tea rooms

Like today's international fast-food chains and coffee shops, tea-room chains thrived on merciless economies of scale. They were heirs to the industrial revolution that replaced small workshops with factories, and kin to giant Indian tea plantations, which triumphed over the tiny tea plots of Chinese farmers. Similarly, Lyons' engineers built immense factories for making the vast amount of food the company served. The daily output of Swiss rolls was measured in miles.

Tea-room chains often provoked ambivalence. In *Angel Pavement* J.B. Priestley contrasted the vigorous enjoyment upstairs where people ate, with the cerebral science of basement statisticians and accountants, who spent their days working with fractions of pennies to trim prices, discovering how much electricity it took to make a steak and kidney pudding and how long the average waitress would take to carry a laden tray from the kitchen to the restaurant. Though Priestley rather scorned the fine-tuned calculations that underpinned Lyons, in fact they were essential: in the 1920s the profit on a full meal at Lyons was reputed to be only one farthing.

Murphy fights the tea-room Goliath

The hero of Samuel Beckett's *Murphy* shares Priestley's disdain. He devotes himself to undermining the calculations of business in a daily battle in which single-handed tactics triumph over fearful odds. 'Only compare the belligerents', he says:

> *On the one hand a colossal league of plutomaniac caterers, highly endowed with the ruthless cunning of the sane, having at their disposal all the most deadly weapons of the post-war recovery; on the other a seedy solipsist and fourpence.*

Armed with his fourpence, Murphy orders:

> *A cup of tea and a packet of assorted biscuits. Twopence the tea, twopence the biscuits, a perfectly balanced meal.*

Murphy begins this lunch 'vitiated by no base thoughts of nutrition', by gulping half the tea, then gagging as if 'duped into swallowing a saturated solution of powdered glass'. When the waitress comes, he tells her that he had ordered China tea, not Indian. Of course, she replaces his half-empty cup of Indian tea with a full cup of China tea. Now Murphy takes a second aim. He drinks a third of the fresh tea, then asks the waitress to fill the cup with hot tea:

> *'I know I am a great nuisance, but they have been too generous with the cowjuice.' Generous and cowjuice were the keywords here. No waitress could hold out against their mingled overtones of gratitude and mammary organs. . . . That is the end of how Murphy defrauded a vested interest every day for his lunch, to the honourable extent of paying for one cup of tea and consuming 1.83 cups approximately.*

Tea and biscuits

After triumphing Murphy retreats to the park with his packet of biscuits. Biscuit factories had been created by companies such as Carr's, Huntley and Palmer's, Peek

Frean's, and Jacob's in the late Nineteenth Century. Their biscuits cost less than the earlier rout or Naples biscuits, which were made by confectioners, and were soon a favourite companion to tea. Murphy's packet includes a Ginger, an Osborne, a Digestive, a Petit Buerre, and 'one anonymous'. Like any biscuit lover, he has his favourites, so the order of eating them is momentous:

> *He always ate the first-named last, because he liked it best, and the anonymous first, because he thought it very likely the least palatable. The order in which he ate the remaining three was indifferent to him and varied irregularly from day to day.*

But Murphy realises that any fixed order of eating 'violates the very essence of assortment' because it provides only six possible variations. Furthermore:

> *Even if he conquered his prejudice against the anonymous there would only be twenty-four ways in which the biscuits could be eaten. But were he to take the final step and overcome his infatuation with the ginger biscuit, the assortment would spring to life before him, dancing the radiant measure of its total permutability, edible in a hundred and twenty ways.*

You are what you eat at tea

Murphy gets to the heart of the charm of tea rooms: customers have favourites. Each visit they return to either a well-loved treat – the toasted teacakes rather than the iced buns, say – or an exacting exercise on which cake to choose. Would the almond slice be nicer than the Eccles cake? Which is lusciously best: a slice of a serious chocolate cake or a fat and frivolous brandy-snap frothing with cream? Any choice almost necessarily excludes the others, making tea as much an exercise in restraint as in indulgence. Even if you're trying to lose weight you can congratulate yourself that though you have eaten one rule-breaking treat, you have denied yourself several others.

In the hands of novelists and playwrights, who chooses what reveals character. Murphy's preference for ginger biscuits (widely shared) indicates his tough pepperiness. Gwendolen's preference for bread and butter rather than cake in Oscar Wilde's *The Importance of Being Earnest* suggests severity that could age into an imperiousness to match her mother's, Lady Bracknell's. In Virginia Woolf's *Mrs Dalloway*, the inner hunger for some of the sweets of life that consumes Miss Kilman manifests itself in her longing for a pink cake when she has tea with Elizabeth in the Army and Navy Stores:

> *Elizabeth rather wondered whether Miss Kilman could be hungry. It was her way of eating, eating then looking again and again at the plate of sugared cakes on the table next them; then, when a lady and child sat down, and the child took the cake, could Miss Kilman really mind it? Yes, Miss Kilman did mind it. She had wanted that cake – the pink one. The pleasure of eating was almost the only pure pleasure left her, and then to be baffled even in that!*

The chocolate éclair that Miss Kilman actually eats seems not to console her, though in similar circumstances Leonora of Barbara Pym's *The Sweet Dove Died* settles quite happily for a coffee éclair. After a trying visit to the dentist she consoles herself that he had not forbidden her to eat, so she could visit a café that served her favourite Swiss pastry swirled with a spaghetti of chestnut worms. Unfortunately, the waitress offers the cake tray to another table first, and the last remaining chestnut cake goes (recipe pp. 145–6). Disgruntled Leonora orders a coffee éclair, which luckily turns out to be almost as delicious. The luscious softness in both the éclair and the chestnut cake suggest both the luxuriousness of Leonora's nature and her lack of substance. When Humphrey, who is courting her, offers her a hearty date and walnut slice in a country tea room, it's no surprise that she disdains it. Readers realise that Leonora and Humphrey will not make a pair. Equally, they realize that Phoebe, her rival for the affections of the younger James, is much less precious, happily settling for tea with him in a country café with plastic tablecloths, artificial flowers, bottles of sauce and a menu that includes fish and chips, thick bread and butter, and lurid cakes with op-art icing.

Waitresses

When Leonora is balked of her chestnut cake, she vents her annoyance on the blameless waitress. Putting up with tantrums has been as much a part of a waitress's job as the drudgery of carrying heavy trays or negotiating the crannies and twisted steps of so many ye-olde tea rooms. Detachment was often the best defence. Vera, who served Murphy's tea and biscuits, exemplifies this, waiting for his order:

> *With such an air of abstraction that he did not feel entitled to regard himself as an element in her situation.*

Nevertheless, in the late Nineteenth and early Twentieth Centuries, being a tea-room waitress was a desirable job compared to working as a servant, whose hours were interminable, or in a factory, where pay was better but the environment dirty and definitely déclassé. Mildred in Somerset Maugham's *Of Human Bondage* certainly thought being a waitress more genteel, but though she infatuates Philip she makes no effort to behave courteously to him or anyone else:

> *She had the art of treating women who desired refreshment with just that degree of impertinence which irritated them*

without affording them an opportunity to complain to the management.

Julia Comstock in George Orwell's *Keep the Aspidistra Flying* works in a tea shop that her brother describes as both nasty and ladylike. It's owned by a family friend who sweet-talks her with pet names, but works her for 72 hours a week for 25 shillings plus her lunch and tea. The veneer of refinement makes the job seem suitable for an impecunious lady, and Julia is too self-sacrificing to complain – or perhaps even notice.

Women in the tea-room business

Vera, Mildred, Julia and their kind well knew the drudgery of tea rooms, yet many women with a little capital thought they could have fun and make money by opening one. Orwell suggested that the Comstock family would have done better to spend its small resources buying Julia her own tea place rather than wasting them on an expensive education for her brother. Notably, when Miss Matty loses all her money in Mrs. Gaskell's *Cranford* she is set up in a small tea-selling business. She rather enjoys it. Indeed, running tea shops and tea rooms gave women an entrée into the business world that typically relegated them to ill-paid jobs like Julia's.

Kate Cranston and The Willow Tea Rooms

The most famous woman tea-room owner was Kate Cranston of Glasgow, and the most celebrated of her four tea rooms was The Willow Tea Rooms in Sauchiehall Street.

Always fastidious, Kate Cranston gave architect Charles Rennie Mackintosh a free hand in The Willow Tea Rooms. He and his wife Margaret Macdonald not only designed the building, but also the famous high-backed chairs, the cutlery, the menus and the waitresses' uniforms and all the other fittings. Inspired by the name of Sauchiehall Street, which means 'marsh of the willows' in Scots, Mackintosh used willow motifs throughout. A stylised willow tree ran from the banister to the ceiling from where it drooped with willowy beads. Little willow-leaf shaped mirrors studded the window and reflected the light. His wife embroidered the curtains with willow trees.

Ye Olde Cosye Tea Rooms and their ilk

While no woman matched Kate Cranston's investment in Mackintosh's art nouveau masterpiece, thousands have created pretty tea rooms bedecked with granny's china, floppy garden blooms, and jams, cakes and pastries from their own kitchens. Often, they retooled their parlours as tea rooms, but equally, old cottages, old mills, or any picturesque building could be used with names such as Ye Olde Cosye Tea Room or The Spinning Wheel Café.

Dorothy Sayers pinpointed the differences between these and their big-chain rivals in *Strong Poison.* Miss Climpson has gone to the fictional town of Windle in the Lake District, to ferret out the reclusive Mrs. Wrayburn. She starts by scoping out the local scene from the vantage of a conveniently positioned tea room. Cataloguing Windle's possibilities, she lists eight possible choices, including a well-established tea room, two rising competitors, one fading establishment, and four that combine serving tea with selling sweets. The most central had an orchestra, comfortable seating and quick waitresses, while Ye Cosye Corner – the best one from Miss Climpson's sleuthing point of view – is staffed by languorous ladies in art-linen. Their languor may well be the result of the long work days exacted by owners such as Julia Comstock's employer in *Keep the Aspidistra Flying.* Unfortunately, Miss Climpson gets no leads at the tea room around which they drift. Success eventually comes her way in The Oriental, whose only eastern element seems to be dim 40-watt bulbs in Japanese shades.

Diva's tea-room venture

When Diva in E.F. Benson's *Trouble for Lucia* opens a tea room in her home, her friends gossip about the pros and cons. Georgie points out advantages other than the financial:

> *She'll enjoy it so much. . .popping in and out and talking to her customers. She's got such a raving passion for talking to anybody, and she finds it such silent work living alone.*

He's right: Diva spends most of her time chatting with her clientèle. Of course, catty Elizabeth Mapp casts aspersions. 'Poor Diva can't make tea ... it's either hot water or pure tannin,' she avers, noting too, that 'She intends to make all the pastry herself. ... Much better to stick to bread and butter and plain cake.' But Diva manages quite well. She offers a shilling tea of bread and butter and pastry fingers with Indian or China tea. For eighteenpence customers also get cream for the tea and potted meat sandwiches (recipe for potted meat, pp. 156–7). Eventually, she also includes 'delicious jam puffs', so her pastry-making skills prove adequate. However, she has a serious problem with the marrow jam that Elizabeth had made:

> *Tea had been brought in. There was a pot of greenish jam, and Elizabeth loaded her buttered toast with it and put it in her mouth. She gave a choking cry and washed it down with a gulp of tea. 'Anything wrong?' asked Diva. 'Yes dear, I am afraid it's fermenting,' said Elizabeth laying down her piece of toast. 'And I can't conceive what it's made of.' Diva*

looked at the pot. 'You ought to know,' she said. 'It's one of those pots you gave me. Labelled vegetable marrow. So sorry it's not eatable.'

This is a neat revenge: whilst renting Diva's house Mapp had used all Diva's raspberries and strawberries to make much tastier jam which she kept for herself, giving Diva only the horrid marrow jam made from the crop of her own garden.

Department store teas

The other alternative to the chain tea rooms were department stores, which realised they could keep women meandering around their many floors by siting a tea room on the least accessible of them – usually the highest.

Some of the most famous department store tea rooms are offshoots of tea merchants. Fortnum and Mason's in Piccadilly began selling tea in 1720, and have always served the clubs and houses of neighbouring Mayfair. Nowadays, shoppers can sip tea while congratulating themselves on their gorgeous purchases in St. James' Restaurant.

Harrods started life as a Stepney grocery that branched into tea when the East India Company lost its monopoly. By the 1880s it was expanding into the Knightsbridge store as we know it, though its slogan then was 'The Cheapest Store in London', with a Ladies Reading Room serving tea with toast, muffins or crumpets.

Tea rooms today

Department store tea rooms still survive, buoyed by shoppers' eternal need for a revitalising sit-down. And tea rooms can be found in even the smallest village, with clusters of them anywhere picturesque enough to draw visitors.

They thrive because few people can now take time for afternoon tea at home; most of us are still at work most of the time. But on a day out or holiday, tea-time is perhaps the more beloved because we can so rarely fit it in to our day. Cream teas with scones and jam plus perhaps some regional favourite such as a toasted tea cake or Eccles cake in the North, a cream-filled split in Devon or Cornwall (recipes, pp. 137–8, 132–3, 142–3, 135–6), celebrate a visit to a favourite place and time off work.

A few tea rooms still have multiple branches. Betty's of Harrogate in Yorkshire was established in 1919 by a Swiss immigrant, and keeps alive its Swiss heritage in its Yorkshire home with its chocolate torte and Engadine torte sitting beside Yorkshire curd tarts, sloe-gin fruitcake, and Betty's signature Fat Rascals: large scones made more luxurious with extra butter, almonds and cherries.

Betty's has branches in York, Skipton, Northallerton and Ilkley, and like the Lyons of yore, has comfortable surroundings with service from waitresses wearing the traditional uniforms. Yet while Betty's and other tea rooms pack in customers, the giant Lyons chain has gone, its name surviving in a brand of tea and in packages of tarts and cakes on supermarket shelves.

Perhaps this shows that one shape of tea room does not fit all. Or merely that marketers of fast food and coffee have snapped up the prime High Street locations that once housed Lyons, Fuller's and others. Even so, a new breed of tea rooms is appearing. Some feature herbal infusions as well as real tea. Others offer Chinese and Japanese teas in pared-down settings inspired by Japanese aesthetics. All point out the recent research that suggests that tea has health benefits. Beyond relieving the four o'clock brownout that drives people into tea rooms, scientists now suggest tea helps lower rates of cancer, cardiovascular disease and tooth decay. Green tea may also protect the skin. So the history of tea circles back to its origins in early

Chinese medicine, when it was prescribed for rheumatism, improving eyesight, relieving asthma and dealing with 'noxious vapours'.

London's Gardens

One of the most exciting ways to take tea in Eighteenth and early Nineteenth-Century London was to visit one of its many pleasure gardens such as twelve-acre Vauxhall Gardens or Ranelagh. Unlike male-only coffee houses and pubs, they welcomed women and families to enjoy the tea pavilions, the entertainers and the fireworks. Leopold Mozart recorded visiting Ranelagh:

> *On entering everyone pays 2s.6d. For this he may have as much bread and butter as he can eat, and as much coffee or tea as he can drink.*

In *Vanity Fair* Thackeray describes Vauxhall with its

> *hundred thousand* extra *lamps, which were always lighted, the fiddlers in cocked hats, who played ravishing melodies ... the dark walks so favourable to young lovers.*

Becky Sharp hopes to entice rich Jos Sedley of the East India Company into marriage, but he drinks himself incapable on rack punch, so no luck for Becky. If only she had persuaded him to take tea! Historian Alan Macfarlane suggests: 'The teashop and the public garden were well suited to the British system of domestic centred companionate marriage.'

Chapter 7

Tea and How to Make It

> *Tea is a work of art. ... There is no single recipe for making the perfect tea, as there are no rules for producing a Titian. ... Each preparation of the leaves has its individuality, its special affinity with water and heat, its hereditary memories to recall, its own method of telling a story.*
>
> Okakura Kakuzo, *The Book of Tea*

Types of tea

All tea comes from the Himalayan plant *Camellia sinensis*. First heard of in China, it thrives in the mountains that straddle neighbouring regions including northern India. In the wild, tea naturally hybridises. Modern botanists recognise three varieties: *Camellia sinensis* var. *sinensis* from China, *Camellia sinensis* var. *assamica*, from Assam, and *Camellia sinensis* var. *cambodi* from Java. In addition, there are hundreds of subvarieties plus modern clones created to suit the conditions of the world's many tea-growing countries.

The tastes of tea

Until the Nineteenth Century Europeans assumed that different teas came from different plants. After all, green tea does not look or taste the same as black tea; the smoky Lapsang Souchong differs from the fresh-tasting Gunpowder;

the flowery jasmine from a brisk Keemun breakfast tea. In fact, processing methods account for most of these differences.

Another significant factor is *terroir* – a French wine-growers' term that pinpoints the combined and mysterious effects of variations in soil, microclimate and the orientation and gradient of the slope where the bushes grow. *Terroir* explains why areas such as Darjeeling, Assam and Kenya excel in black teas, but do not produce the finest green teas. Conversely, the most prestigious green teas come from China and Japan.

Plucking tea

Left to itself tea grows into a tree, but cultivated tea is trimmed into waist-high bushes to make plucking easier.

Tea is an evergreen. Nonetheless, in China it has a distinct growing season with new leaves appearing from spring to late autumn. Its new growth signalled spring for the poet Po Chu-I:

The ice breaks and the snow begins to melt.
On the southern plantations the tea plant thrusts its sprouts;
Through the northern crevice the veins of the spring ooze.

The earliest buds to unfurl are called 'the first flush' and they make the finest black and green teas as well as white tea. Other pluckings occur throughout the season, including, when possible, during the monsoon, until the bush returns to dormancy.

The Assamese variety of tea, which grows in India, Sri Lanka and Africa, likes high temperatures and humidity, preferably with alternating dry and rainy spells. Since it grows in the tropics, it produces leaves throughout the year.

Tea bushes are never stripped bare. Only the new tips including the bud or first baby leaflets and the two bigger leaves behind it are picked, though additional leaves may be used in some teas, and a few Japanese teas include selected snips of twig.

Though tea-picking has been mechanised, especially when the tea is to be processed for mass-market tea bags, the finest teas are still plucked by hand. Chinese tea connoisseurs value tea leaves, both when dried and when brewed, for their beauty, so pickers take great care when plucking, and skilled artisans roll or twist the leaves into the shapes characteristic of each kind of tea.

Processing and different kinds of tea

Before tea leaves can be brewed into cups of tea, they must be dried and in the case of black teas, oxidised. The processing, all of which takes place in the tea gardens, accounts for a myriad of differences among varieties of tea, and while the drying or withering the leaves is the fundamental step, minute and complex variations in method create major differences in the final product.

1. **White tea**: Only the buds and the first tender leaves with silvery hairs on their underside are used for white tea. Grown in the Fujian province of China, white tea is protected from the sun to limit chlorophyll development, and dried quickly, without heat. White tea has barely any colour and the most delicate flavours.
2. **Green tea:** Leaves are picked early in the day and immediately left to wither, first in the air then on mats. They must dry quickly and thoroughly to preserve their greenness, so they are lightly toasted or tossed in baskets exposed briefly to heat. The leaves are rolled or twisted to create a variety of intriguing

shapes. Japanese green tea develops its characteristic flavour because it is also briefly steamed.

3. **Yellow tea:** This rare Chinese tea, once grown only for the Imperial court, is processed like green tea, but steamed then rested under covers to preserve its flavours before it is withered. The brewed tea is yellow with hints of walnut flavour.
4. **Oolong:** A speciality of Taiwan and eastern China, oolong tea is the halfway state between unoxidised green tea and oxidised black tea. Its processing is complex, and involves shaking and tumbling the leaves several times to bruise them so they oxidise just a little. Ultimately, oxidisation ranges from 35 per cent to 80 per cent, canting some oolongs towards green tea while others edge towards black tea. The colour of brewed oolong ranges correspondingly from maize through amber to chestnut.
5. **Black tea:** Most westerners drink black tea. The leaves are withered, rolled, oxidised and dried. Oxidisation occurs in airy rooms, where the leaves become dark brown or black after absorbing oxygen that transforms their chemistry and creates new flavour compounds. Lapsang Souchong is lightly smoked, typically exported rather than drunk by the Chinese who make it. Traditionally, skilled artisans roll or twist tea leaves. Today, vast amounts are processed in cut-tear-curl (CTC) machines so that juices are quickly released on brewing, making them suitable for mass-market teas, especially tea bags. Black tea is sorted into many grades. Some of the most important follow:

   - Flowery Orange Pekoe: high quality tea made from the bud and one new leaf.
   - Golden Flowery Orange Pekoe: includes the paler buds that do not darken during processing.

- Tippy Golden Flowery Orange Pekoe: like golden orange pekoe with more tips.
- Finest Tippy Golden Flowery Orange Pekoe: excellent quality with lots of tips.
- Orange Pekoe: long leaves picked just as buds open.
- Pekoe: shorter leaves than orange pekoe.

6. **Pu'erh tea.** Unlike other Chinese teas, pu'erh tea is made from the Assamese plant *Camellia sinensis* var. *assamica*, so it has the colour and strength of Indian or Kenyan tea. After drying, the leaves are remoistened, encouraging the action of naturally occurring bacteria. This causes fermentation, which results in new properties and flavours. Pu'erh may be sold as loose tea, but often it is compressed into cakes and paper-wrapped for storage. As the cakes mature they mellow and develop rather beefy or Marmite-like aromas. Some pu'erh is aged for decades, increasing in flavour – and cost – all the time. Many infusions can be made from a small amount of pu'erh tea. It aids digestion and some Chinese believe it prevents obesity.
7. **Compressed tea.** Pu'erh is but one form of compressed tea. Black, green and oolong teas can also be compressed, a technique developed centuries ago because cakes of tea were easier to carry to distant Central Asia than bulky loose tea. The tea was mixed with plum juice or other liquid, then pressed into moulds that left grooves so it could be split into pieces like a bar of chocolate. When needed, a bit was broken off, warmed until soft, then ground to a powder and brewed.
8. **Flavoured teas.** Tea readily absorbs flavours and the Chinese have perfected the art of making flower-scented teas. Jasmine and rose-scented teas are the best-known, but orchids, honeysuckle, chrysanthemums, marigold, gardenia and lotus-blossoms are among

the many flowers that have been used. Fourteenth-Century instructions for preparing lotus tea show the Chinese efforts expended in the interest of flavour:

> *In the pond, before breakfast, as the sun rises, choose slightly opened lotus buds. Separate the petals with your fingers and put in tea leaves, filling them up. Tie with a piece of rope. Wait overnight, then pick the lotus next morning, remove the tea, wrap it in paper and let it dry. Repeat it for three times. Put it in a tin container to store.*

Presentation flower teas are made from bundles of leaves tied around a dried flower, and formed into marble-size balls or heart shapes. In hot water the leaves expand into a chrysanthemum-like mop, and the pink or yellow flower in the centre blooms again.

Fragrant fruits such as lychees and oranges can also scent tea. Earl Grey tea is flavoured with bergamot, a small variety of orange. Other popular flavourings include mint, used in many Arab countries, and the array of spices, including cardamom, cinnamon and cloves in Indian *masala chai*.

Herbal infusions

Tea scented with flowers or fruit differs from infusions made solely from flowers, leaves or fruit from plants other than *Camellia sinensis*. Though often miscalled 'tea', these are herbal infusions or *tisanes*. A lime-flower *tisane* may have sparked the flood of memory that sets off the record of a life in Proust's *Remembrance of Things Past*:

> *The taste was that of the little crumb of Madeleine which on Sunday mornings at Combray ... my Aunt Leonie used to give me, dipping it first in her own cup of real or lime-flower tea.*

The Queen of Camellias

The tea bush *Camellia sinensis* belongs to the camellia family. Dried tea leaves of *Camellia sinensis* arrived in Europe by the early Seventeenth Century. Its garden cousins came later, brought by Eighteenth and Nineteenth-Century botanists who travelled the east in search of lovely flowers, bringing chrysanthemums, peonies, Chinese roses and Japanese anemones as well as camellias to the west. Like these, the tea plant will bloom, but its pretty yellowy-white flower rarely appears as the growing tips are picked before it blossoms. When it appears its seeds are valued because they yield an oil used in some cooked dishes, such as the soup described on p. 14. Like tea itself, this edible teaseed oil is entirely different from the inedible tea tree oil of the Australian plant *Malaleuca alternifolia,* which is unrelated to *Camellia sinensis.*

Many varieties: lovely names

With a kaleidoscope of factors, including the variety of the tea, where it's grown, how it's processed and whether it's handmade or mass-produced all contributing to the colour, appearance and flavour, tea producers and retailers have had to conjure up thousands of names for their products. Among the most evocative are Jasmine Pearl – silvery leaves rolled into pearl-size balls deliciously scented with jasmine – Gunpowder tea shaped in shot-like grey pellets and Fairy Ladies' Golden Rings, which comes as tiny rings, just about fairy size, that make a golden tea. Butterfly in Love has knotted leaves that look like butterflies – more or less – when immersed in water. Other pretty names include

Dragon Eye, Iron Goddess Of Mercy, White Monkey Paw, Kyoto Cherry Rose, White Snow Buds and Five Golden Flowers.

Tea bags

The biggest Twentieth-Century development in tea was the invention of the tea bag by the American tea merchant Thomas Sullivan. In 1908 he sent samples to customers in silk pouches rather than the usual paper packets. Instead of emptying them, some recipients assumed the bag was a filter and simply dropped the whole thing into their pot. Inspired by this, Sullivan moved on to gauze bags that made better infusions. By the 1920s two sizes of gauze and paper bags were being produced commercially: big bags for the pot, smaller ones for the cup.

Tea bags did not reach Britain until the 1950s, when the end of rationing enabled tea companies to experiment with packaging. Welcoming arms did not immediately greet the tea bag. In *Travels with my Aunt* Graham Greene describes an American couple having tea in Paris:

> *One of them was raising a little bag, like a drowned animal, from his cup at the end of a cord. At that sight I felt very far away from England.*

Now nothing could be commoner than the sight of a tea bag. In the early 1960s, less than 3 per cent of Britain's tea came in bags; in 2007 the figure was 96 per cent. Companies vie for buyers with shapes varying from square to round to pyramidal; some bags have strings and dangly labels; others come in their own little packets. The latest are 'silken' – actually a mixture of nylon and silk with excellent infusing properties and more like Thomas Sullivan's silk pouches than Greene's 'drowned animal' bags.

Tasting and blending tea

All the tea in tea bags as well as supermarket packets of loose tea and indeed some speciality teas are blends. The flavours of each brand of tea differ because each brand is a mix of ten or fifteen teas. To keep their loyal customers, tea companies must ensure that variations in the harvest or processing don't cause variations in the flavour. Thus, their tea tasters constantly sample teas sent by the growers, seeking tastes and flavours characteristic of their company's blend.

When packages of tea arrive from the gardens, tasters brew it in special vessels for 3–5 minutes depending on the tea. A lid covers it until brewing is complete, then the whole thing is inverted so the liquid runs out into a bowl-shaped cup. The leaves remain on the lid, which is displayed so the taster can observe their appearance.

As for the tea itself, tasters suck in a spoonful through their teeth and swish it round with sucky-slurpy noises – the sort that children are forbidden to make – that let the tea release its aromas and bathe every taste bud. The taster notes smells, flavours and tastes such as bitter, sour and sweet. Like wine experts, tea tasters have their own vocabulary to describe what they taste. Desirable characteristics include the following:

- Astringent: a drying effect, which, balanced by other characteristics, is satisfyingly thirst-quenching.
- Biscuity: used of Assamese tea to indicate the malty flavour characteristic of the region's tea.
- Brisk: used of well-made teas with good astringency.
- Clean: clear flavour with no unpleasant components.
- Full: a well-made tea with strength and rounded flavour.
- Pointy or bright: clear-tasting refreshing tea.
- Soft: the opposite of brisk in tea terms, indicating smoothness rather than vigour.

In contrast, words such as 'muddy', 'coarse', 'metallic' or 'thin' indicate that the processing of the tea has been poor so it doesn't taste satisfying or pleasant.

Orwell on how not to make tea

In his 1946 *Evening Standard* article *A Nice Cup of Tea,* George Orwell noted that tea is a mainstay of British life, yet 'violent disputes' could break out over how to make it. He was right. Most people agree on using boiling water, warming the pot, taking the pot to the kettle rather than vice versa, and vigorous stirring before letting the tea brew. But should sugar be added? Orwell opposed it because it spoiled the bitter taste that helps make tea invigorating. He also thumbs-downed cream in tea because it makes tea taste sickly. As for the perennial question: should the milk go in the cup first, or after the tea has been poured? Orwell believed he had defeated the milk-first battalion with the argument that if it goes in last, the drinker can judge exactly how much to add by the colour of the tea. But on this battlefield, the milk-first warriors have the undeniable argument that as the hot tea hits the milk, it changes the flavour, creating a more fully-rounded taste. Moreover, history is on their side. When the English first added milk to tea in the late Seventeenth Century, putting milk in the cup first cut the risk that the boiling water would crack the fragile cups of those days.

Boiling water?

But should the water be boiling? The most sacrosanct British rule insists on boiling water – not water that has recently boiled or is just off the boil. Yet the boiling-water rule does not hold universal sway. Americans rarely follow it. With ordinary supermarket teas the result is disastrous, but with green teas and quality handmade teas using water just off the boil is better because boiling water can make them too astringent. Tea experts suggest white and green teas be made with water at around 80ºC, oolong at 90ºC or a little more, black tea at around 95ºC and only pu'erh tea with boiling water.

As for the water itself, water fresh-drawn from the tap, not water that has stood around in the kettle, makes better tea because it is more oxygenated. Should your tap water be hard, buy teas blended for hard water. If it has too many chemical additives, choose still mineral water.

Teapot or mug?

Tea is best made in a teapot. As well as looking lovely, teapots are big enough to let the leaves swell in the water and release their flavour. As for keeping tea leaves out of the cup, use a pot with a spout fitted with a strainer or pour it through a strainer perched on the cup. Ball-type tea infusers are not a good idea because they don't let the leaves expand fully.

As for mugs, the ease with which a tea bag can be dropped in and fished out is a major selling point for tea bags. Yet even in a mug, tea should be covered (with a saucer for example) while it is brewing. Covering the cup or the pot makes the tea taste better. China mugs are better than thick earthenware ones because the tea tastes better out of them – just as wine tastes better from a thin glass rather than a beer mug. An added benefit is that bone china is less fragile than thick earthenware, despite appearances to the contrary.

Brewing tea

Don't let the tea stand in the water too long. As early as 1669, Sir Kenelm Digby noted that a tea drinker with experience in China had told him, 'We let the hot water remain too long soaking upon the Tea'. This extracted 'the earthy parts of the herb'. Tea poured after just 3–4 minutes brewing has 'only the spiritual parts of the Tea, which is much more active, penetrating and friendly to nature'. Indeed, once brewed tea should be poured, and a second infusion made with fresh water. Green tea, oolong, pu'erh and many fine black teas can yield several infusions.

Reading the tea leaves

After tea has reached the end of its journey from the tropical slopes where it grows, across the oceans and finally into the cup, one last step may remain after savouring it: tasseography – reading the tea leaves.

When the tea is in the cup a floating tea leaf warns of a stranger coming. If the leaf is soft, the stranger is a woman; if woody, it's a man. Tea dripped into a saucer signals a kind nature, perhaps because it symbolises an overflowing heart as Harriet Vane suggests in Dorothy L. Sayers' *Busman's Honeymoon.*

For more detailed readings, the last dregs of the tea are swirled round the cup and the liquid discarded. The reader then looks at the shapes suggested by the leaves starting with those on the rim by the handle. Interpretations are many: a heart foretells happiness; two hearts presage a marriage. A ring at the bottom of a cup means separation. Leaves dotted round the side suggest money. An envelope shape predicts good news. A snake means enmity. A flower shape means children will bring happiness.

Tea-leaf readers have their whims. In Graham Greene's *Travels with my Aunt*, Aunt Augusta's Brighton friend Hattie offers an expert reading, saying:

> *I'll make another pot. The leaves have to be fresh and I use Lapsang Souchong professionally, though I drink Ceylon –*

> *Lapsang give big leaves and good results. . . . I don't let the tea draw, the leaves speak better fresh.*

As she examines the first cup, a name previously lost to memory suddenly pops into her head:

> *I often notice that with the leaves. Things come back. You are watching the leaves and things come back.*

Senior moments thus join the many ailments that tea can relieve.

Chapter 8

Tea and Tea-time Recipes

Tea-Time Breads Large and Small

Muffins

In the Nineteenth Century muffins starred on tea tables the way scones do today. Many writers, including Charles Dickens, Charlotte Brontë, and Beatrix Potter evoke them appreciatively, though George Bernard Shaw complained that they failed to provide inspiration.

350ml/12 fl oz/1½ cups milk

35g/1¼oz/3 tbsp butter

15g/½oz/1 tbsp dried yeast

75ml/2½ fl oz/3 cups warm water

1 tbsp honey

1 egg, lightly beaten

2 tsp salt

1 tbsp vinegar

About 750g/1½ lb/5 cups plain flour

2–3 tbsp fine polenta or cornflour

Warm the milk and butter together until the butter melts. Cool to blood heat. Mix the yeast with the warm water and stir in the honey; leave for about 5 minutes or until frothy. Mix with the milk and butter, then stir in the egg, salt and vinegar. Put half the flour in the mixing bowl, make a well in the centre, pour in the liquid ingredients, and mix (preferably using an electric mixer) for about 2–3 minutes (longer if working by hand), until you have a smooth dough. Mix in the remaining flour, a little at a time until the dough is stiff, and knead for 5 minutes or until it no longer sticks to your hands. Cover the bowl with cling film, and leave in a draught-free spot for about an hour or until doubled in bulk. Shake the polenta or cornflour onto a plate. Divide the dough into 10–12 portions and flatten them into 3-inch circles. Sit each in the polenta or cornflour to dry the bottom and place on a dry tray. Cover with a tea towel. Let rise until doubled: about 25 minutes. Bake on a lightly greased griddle or nonstick frying pan over medium heat. They need 5–6 minutes per side. Turn them gently so they remain puffy. They are ready when brown but yielding to slight pressure in the middle. Split with a fork so you leave a rough surface that will absorb lots of butter.

DERBYSHIRE TEA CAKES

On her arrival in North Yorkshire, Ailsa of Margaret Drabble's *The Sea Lady*, orders herself tea with a tea cake. Yorkshire tea cakes, common well beyond the county borders, come studded with dried fruit. But in *Recipes from an Old Farmhouse* Alison Uttley, author of the *Little Grey Rabbit* books, remembers tea cakes made on the Derbyshire farm where she grew up. They were usually plain, she writes, but 'sometimes we had candied peel or spice'. Spice makes the aroma of toasted tea cakes alluring, and in this recipe based on Alison Uttley's the candied peel adds chewy moments of flavour.

1 tbsp dried yeast

425ml/15 fl oz/1¾ cups warm milk

700g/1½ pounds/6 cups strong flour

4oz muscovado sugar

½ tsp salt

½ tsp mace or freshly grated nutmeg

½ tsp allspice

¼ tsp cinnamon

115g/4oz/1 stick melted but cool butter

85g/3oz/about ¾ cup candied peel

Mix the yeast into the warm milk and let it stand while you mix the flour, sugar, salt, mace, allspice and cinnamon in a large bowl. Make a well in the centre, and pour in the yeasty milk, then the butter. Mix and knead, either in an electric mixer or by hand, to form a smooth dough. Cover the bowl with plastic and let rise in a warm place until doubled in bulk: about 1½ hours. Flatten the dough into a rectangle. Scatter about half the candied peel on top then roll it up. Turn it a quarter of a turn, flatten it again – a few bashes with a rolling pin does the job – then scatter on the remaining candied peel. Roll it up again, then knead to distribute the peel evenly. Divide into 12 portions; form each into a ball, and set on a baking sheet, greased or lined with parchment. Cover and let double in bulk, which takes about 45 minutes. Pre-heat the oven to 200°C (400°F). Bake the tea cakes for 15–18 minutes or until they sound hollow when rapped on the bottom.

BARA BRITH

Nothing is more traditional in Britain than festive breads or cakes with dried fruit. Arnold Bennett lists raisin-bread and currant-bread among the array 'which differentiates high tea from tea'. Most regions have a local fruit bread, though they vary only slightly. In Wales it's bara brith, which means 'speckled bread'. The dried fruit makes the speckles.

225g/8oz mixed dried fruit

55g/2oz/⅓ cup candied peel

1 cup strong brewed tea

115g/4oz/1 stick butter

2 tbsp golden syrup or treacle

350g/12oz/3 cups plain flour

2 tsp baking powder

85g/3oz/½ cup muscovado sugar

½ tsp freshly grated nutmeg

2 eggs, lightly beaten

Put the dried fruit and the peel in a small bowl with the tea. Leave overnight or for at least 6 hours. Pre-heat the oven to 180°C (350°F) and line a 22.5cm × 12.5cm (9 × 5 inch) loaf tin with parchment or grease it. In a small pan, melt the butter with the syrup or treacle. In a large bowl mix the flour, baking powder, sugar and nutmeg. Make a well in the centre and add the lightly beaten egg and the butter mixture. Mix well then stir in the fruit and tea. Turn into the prepared tin and bake for 30 minutes. Reduce the temperature to 160°C (325°F) and bake for another 50–60 minutes or until a skewer inserted in the centre comes out clean. Let cool in the pan on a rack. Keep wrapped when cool.

Buns

In J.B. Priestley's *Angel Pavement* Turgis watches women happily eating cream buns in the big tea shop where he goes for his fortnightly evening treat. Here's the basic bun recipe with variations for currant buns, cream buns and Bath buns.

225ml/8 fl oz/1 cup milk

1 tbsp yeast

55g/2oz/¼ cup sugar

450g/1 lb flour/4 cups (or a little more)

½ tsp salt

55g/2oz/4 tbsp butter, melted

Warm the milk to blood heat. Mix 3 tablespoons of it with the yeast and a teaspoon of the sugar. Mix the flour, remaining sugar and salt in a large bowl. Make a well in the centre, and when the yeast froths, pour it in. Add the remaining milk and melted butter. Knead with a dough hook of an electric mixer or by hand until the dough loses its stickiness. Shape into a ball; place in a large bowl; cover and set in a warm, draught-free spot until doubled in bulk: about an hour. Turn the oven to 220°C (425°F). Grease a baking tray or line it with parchment paper. Punch down the dough; knead for a minute or so, then divide it into 10 pieces. Roll each into a ball and put on the baking tray. Cover them with cling film and let rise until doubled again: about 25 minutes. Bake for 18–20 minutes or until golden and hollow-sounding when rapped on the bottom. Cool on a wire cooling rack.

To make Cream Buns (sometimes called Devonshire Splits): cut the buns slantwise, from the top right to the bottom left, without severing the two halves. Open and spread strawberry or raspberry jam on the bottom then load with whipped or clotted cream. Dust with icing sugar for serving.

To make Currant Buns: add 1 teaspoon of mixed spice to the flour and sugar. After you punch down the dough, flatten it, scatter on 55g (2oz) ⅓ cup currants and knead them in. When they come out of the oven boil 2 tablespoons of sugar with 2 tablespoons of milk until bubbly, then while the buns are still hot, brush the surface for a shiny glaze.

To make Bath Buns: increase the butter to 115g (4oz/ 1 stick). Beat an egg (and, if you like, a teaspoon of caraway seeds) into the warm milk before adding it. Make the buns flattish rather than domed, and place only an inch apart on the baking sheet so they touch when baked. While they bake, crush 8–10 sugar cubes into tiny chunks. When the buns are just out of the oven, make a glaze by boiling 3 tablespoons of white sugar with 2 tablespoons of milk in a small pan until very bubbly. Immediately brush it on the hot buns. Scatter some crushed sugar cubes on top.

CINNAMON TOAST

Toast browned before a red fire is to toast popped from a toaster as the burned sausages hot from the poker that Harry Potter eats at tea with Hagrid are to ordinary sausages from a frying pan. The touch of the living flame makes all the difference to the aroma. Charlotte Brontë's Jane Eyre loves the smell of toast: 'How fragrant was the steam of the beverage, and the scent of the toast!' she thinks when she visits Miss Temple. Notably, when Miss Temple asks for more toast, she refers to it as 'bread and butter', suggesting that some of the many Nineteenth-Century references to tea-time bread and butter may actually be to toast. Cinnamon Toast has long been beloved of children and anyone with a sweet tooth.

3 tsp caster sugar

1 tsp cinnamon

2 slices bread, white or wholemeal

butter

Turn on the grill (broiler). Mix the sugar and cinnamon. Toast the bread quite lightly, and butter it. Sprinkle on the sugar and cinnamon mixture in an even layer. Place under the grill, and watching carefully so it doesn't burn, toast it until the sugar has melted and the surface looks glossy and maybe has a bubble or two. Remove and eat immediately, cut in fingers if you like.

Scones, Biscuits and Small Cakes

SULTANA SCONES

In May Sinclair's *The Cure of Souls* Canon Chamberlain rarely resists anything he enjoys. Certainly, 'Never in all his life had he been able to resist home-made scones, hot-buttered'. Rosie in Somerset Maugham's *Cakes and Ale* loves them too. Known in Scotland from at least the Sixteenth Century, scones did not flourish on English tea tables until the early 1900s, when they began to edge out buttered muffins.

280g/10oz/2 cups plain flour

1 tbsp baking powder

¼ tsp freshly grated nutmeg

85g/3oz/6 tbsp chilled butter

115g/4oz/½ cup sugar

115g/4oz/ ½ cup sultanas or mixed dried fruit

1 egg, lightly beaten

about 125ml/4 fl oz/ ½ cup milk, preferably sour

Pre-heat the oven to 200°C (400°F) and cover a baking sheet with parchment paper or grease it. In a large bowl mix the flour, baking powder and nutmeg. Cut the butter in small pieces and rub them into the flour. Stir in the sugar and then the sultanas or dried fruit. Make a well in the centre and stir in the egg and then the milk to make a stiff dough, adding more milk a tablespoonful at a time as needed to achieve this. Divide it into 8 portions and shape each into 5cm (2-inch) circles about 2cm (¾ inch) thick. Place on the baking sheet and bake for 15–20 minutes or until golden brown.

To make Cherry Scones: use glacé cherries instead of sultanas, replace 2 tablespoons of the flour with 2 tablespoons ground almonds and add ¼ teaspoon almond essence.

To make Apricot-Almond Scones: substitute 15 dried and soaked apricots each cut in bits, 2 tablespoons of ground almonds and ¼ teaspoon almond essence. Sprinkle a few flaked almonds on top before baking.

COCONUT CAKES

In Mrs. Gaskell's *North and South* coconut cakes are a Hale family speciality, while in P.L. Travers' *Mary Poppins* they are one of Uncle Albert's birthday treats.

175g/6oz/1½ cups plain flour

1 tsp baking powder

115g/4oz butter/1 stick butter, softened

115g/4oz/ ½ cup sugar

2 eggs

1 tbsp dark rum

115g/4oz/1½ cups sweetened dessicated coconut

Pre-heat the oven to 180°C (350°F) and grease two 12-cup sets of patty tins or fairy cake tins. Mix the flour and baking powder, and set aside. In a large bowl beat the butter and sugar until light in colour. Beat in 1 egg and the rum, followed by half the flour. Separate the other egg, reserving the white but mixing the yolk plus 3½ ounces of the coconut into the mixture. Finally, thoroughly blend in the rest of the flour. Divide the mixture among the patty pans letting it mound in the centre. Lightly froth the egg white with a fork, then brush a little onto each cake and sprinkle with some of the remaining coconut. Bake for 18–20 minutes or until golden.

JESSIE CONRAD'S LEMONY TEA CAKES

In his introduction to his wife's 1923 cookery book, *A Handbook of Cookery for a Small House,* Joseph Conrad said her cooking 'has been for many priceless years adding to the sum of my daily happiness'. These tea cakes adapted from Jessie Conrad's recipe are like rich scones rather than the Derbyshire tea cakes on page 132.

280g/10oz/2½ cups plain flour

1 tsp baking powder

6oz butter, soft but not melted

1 egg plus 1 yolk

55g/2oz/½ cup sugar

grated zest of 1 lemon

125ml/4 fl oz/½ cup double cream

Pre-heat the oven to 190°C (375°F) and grease a baking tray. In a large bowl, mix the flour and baking powder. Make a well in the centre and add the butter, the egg, the yolk, sugar, lemon zest and all but 2 tablespoons of the cream, (which will be used for brushing the tops later). Stir to mix, then blend with your hands. Chill in the fridge for 30 minutes, then on a lightly floured board, roll the dough out to 2.5cm (1-inch) thick. Cut into 5cm (2-inch) rounds and place apart on the tray. Brush the tops with the leftover cream and bake for 20–25 minutes.

RASPBERRY JAM CAKES

When Mary Poppins spends an afternoon with her friend the Match Man, he has no money to buy her favourite raspberry jam cakes. Yet a pile as high as Mary's waist magically appears at tea. 'We're having them after all,' Mary exults.

225g/8oz/2 sticks butter at room temperature

115g/4oz/½ cup sugar

2 eggs, separated

1 tsp vanilla essence

280g/10oz/2½ cups plain flour

115g/4oz/1 cup finely chopped walnuts or pecans

about 115g/4oz/¾ cup raspberry jam

In a large bowl, beat the butter and sugar until fluffy. Beat in the egg yolks one at a time, then add the vanilla and about half the flour, and mix well. Finally beat in the rest of the flour. Turn the dough onto a sheet of cling film; wrap it and chill for about 45 minutes. Turn the oven to 160°C

(325°F) and cover two baking sheets with parchment paper. Beat the egg whites on a plate until they foam slightly. Spread the chopped nuts on another plate. Shape pieces of the dough into balls the size of big walnuts. Roll each briefly in the egg white then the nuts. Place it on the baking sheet. Poke your finger in the middle and wiggle it to make a cavity: the raspberry jam will go in later and you want to have a decent space for it. Bake for 15–20 minutes, or until the nuts have darkened slightly and the cakes are gold underneath. While still warm, fill the holes with raspberry jam. (If you fill a few with apricot jam or lemon curd they make a pretty contrast to the raspberry ones.)

BRANDY-SNAPS

In *Anne of Green Gables,* Marilla tells Anne that she can 'have some of the cookies and snaps' when Diana comes to tea. *The Early Canadian Galt Cook Book,* popular when *Anne of Green Gables* was published in 1908, has two recipes for snaps – which we know better as brandy-snaps – from which this one is adapted. They are not as fiddly to shape as they sound, but you can't work with more than a few at a time.

115g/4oz/1 stick butter

115g/4oz golden syrup

115g/4oz sugar

115g/4oz plain flour

2 tsp ground ginger

½ tsp powdered allspice

¼ tsp cloves

2 tsp lemon juice

Turn the oven to 190ºC (375ºF) and put a silicone mat or parchment on a large baking sheet. Melt the butter, syrup and sugar over low heat. When the mixture returns to lukewarm, stir in the flour a little at a time along with the ginger, allspice, cloves and lemon juice. Drop by teaspoonsful on to the prepared sheet. Fit only 6–7 to a sheet as they spread far and wide. Bake for 9–10 minutes, watching carefully during the last minute or two to make sure they don't burn. They are ready when the centre is the colour of caramels, and the edge just a bit darker. Cool only for a minute, while you grease the handle of a wooden spoon. Lift each brandy snap with a palette knife and shape into a cylinder by wrapping it around the greased spoon handle. Slide it off onto a cooling rack with the seam side up so the cylinder doesn't collapse on itself. This must be done quite quickly while they are still soft. If they get too crisp to shape into snaps, warm them in the oven until they are tender again. Store in an airtight tin. If you want to fill them with whipped cream, do so just before serving.

ECCLES CAKES

Round pastry cakes filled with dried fruit come from both Chorley and Banbury, but the version from Eccles uses sugar-crusted puff pastry, making it richer, plumper and popular way beyond its Lancashire home town. The Sunday school children in Arnold Bennett's *Anna of the Five Towns* got Eccles cakes plus currant cake and Bath buns in their bags of tea-time goodies – a triple helping of the dried fruit confections so typical of English festive fare.

70g/2½oz/5 tbsp butter

175g/6oz/1 cup currants

70g/2½oz/2 tbsp candied peel

55g/2oz/¼ cup sugar, plus extra for sprinkling

½ tsp allspice

¼ tsp mace

¼ tsp grated nutmeg

500g/1 lb 2oz/17½oz packet frozen puff pastry

1 egg white

Pre-heat the oven to 220°C (425°F). Place a silicone mat or parchment paper on a baking tray. Put the butter in a small saucepan and let it melt, then stir in the currants, peel, sugar, allspice, mace and nutmeg. Let cool in the fridge while you roll out the puff pastry. Cut it in eight circles using a 14cm (5½-inch) diameter saucer as a guide. To re-use trimmings, stack them and re-roll rather than squishing them into a ball as this preserves the layering of the pastry. Fill each circle with a couple of dessertspoons of the cold filling. Lightly froth the egg white on a plate. Brush the edges of the pastry and then fold over to enclose the filling, making sure there are no gaps. With the folded side facing you, roll each cake a little to make 8cm (3¼ inch) cakes. Put these seam side down on the baking sheet. Brush the surface with egg white and sprinkle half a teaspoon of sugar on each one. Make three cuts, each about 2cm (¾ inch) in the centre to release steam. Bake for 12–15 minutes. Cool on a wire rack. Best slightly reheated for serving.

GREENIES

Intensely chocolatey brownies, though popular, are better with coffee than with tea. But when white chocolate replaces dark chocolate and powdered green tea replaces cocoa, they abracadabra brownies into greenies – perfect with tea, and, on first taste, a bit mysterious, too, since it's hard to guess the secret of these green squares.

85g/3oz/¾ stick unsalted butter

200g/7oz white chocolate

70g/2½ ounces/⅔ cup plain flour

1 tsp baking powder

1 tbsp Japanese green tea powder

pinch salt

2 eggs, lightly beaten

70g/2½ ounces/⅓ cup sugar

1 tbsp brandy or dark sherry

55g/2oz/¼ cup pine nuts

Pre-heat the oven at 180°C (350°F) and line a 20cm (8-inch) square pan with parchment or grease and flour it. Melt the butter and white chocolate either in a microwave, a double boiler or in a bowl placed over a pan of simmering water; (don't let the base of the bowl touch the water). In a bowl stir together the flour, baking powder, green tea and salt. In a small bowl mix the eggs with the sugar and brandy or sherry. Stir half this mixture into the butter and chocolate, then add about a quarter of the flour mixture. When everything is thoroughly blended, stir in more of the flour mixture, then the remaining egg mixture and finally the last of the flour mixture. Be sure to mix thoroughly after each addition. Transfer the batter (which will look a dreary shade of green but don't worry) into the prepared pan. Scatter the pine nuts over the top. Bake for 20–30 minutes or until lightly browned. Test by sticking a skewer or toothpick into the centre. When it comes out clean, the greenies are ready. Cool on a wire rack then loosen the edges and remove from the pan. Cut into 16 squares for serving.

CHESTNUT CAKES

In *The Sweet Dove Died* Barbara Pym uses tea-time choices to characterise Leonora: she refuses a homey date and walnut slice in a country tea shop, but in London she longs for an elegant chestnut cake: a light base topped with 'worms of chestnut purée'. The chestnut worms are easy to make with a piping bag and tinned chestnut cream or purée. The foundation could be meringue nests. Filled with chestnut and topped with cream, they would make mini-Mont Blancs, a classic French dessert. But the foundation could also be sponge cake – as in this recipe. Chestnut cream is lighter than chestnut purée. Both are imported from France and Spain.

2 eggs

115g/4oz/½ cup caster sugar

35g/1¼oz/2 tbsp unsalted butter

¼ tsp vanilla essence

70g/2½oz/½ cup plain flour

¼ tsp baking powder

55g/2oz chestnut cream

225g/8oz sweetened chestnut purée

whipped cream

To garnish: grated dark chocolate, candied violets or raspberries

Pre-heat the oven to 190°C (375°F). Thoroughly grease a 12-cup cupcake or muffin sheet. In a large bowl, whisk the eggs and sugar until they foam and swell about 5 times in bulk. The beater – ideally electric – should leave trails in the mixture. This takes about 7 minutes, during which time you should warm the butter until it melts, then let it cool but not resolidify. Stir it into the egg mixture along with the vanilla, then gently fold in half the flour and the baking powder. When mixed, fold in the rest of the flour. Fill each cupcake cup ⅓ full. Bake for 12–15 minutes or until pale gold. A poked-in skewer should come out clean. Cool for 5 minutes, then remove each cakelet to a rack to finish cooling. Chill before topping. To finish, spread a little chestnut cream on each one, then make chestnut worms by piping the purée through a piping bag fitted with a round nozzle. Chestnut purée is usually very sweet, so no need to completely cover the cake with worms. (If you don't have a piping bag, pack the purée into the corner of a plastic freezer bag fitted with a tip.) Chill until time to serve, then top with a whirl of whipped cream and a tiny garnish: grated chocolate, a berry, candied violets or what you will.

Large Cakes

RUM-RAISIN BATTER CAKE

At tea-time in Anthony Trollope's *Rachel Ray* Rachel regularly delights her mother by running to a nearby farm for 'a little thick cream, and there would be a batter cake'. This puddingy cake is not as rich as Rachel's, which was made of clotted cream, but compensates with rum-flavoured raisins or sultanas.

125g/4oz/1 cup raisins or sultanas

2 tbsp dark rum

1 tsp baking powder

85g/3oz/¾ cup plain flour

85g/3oz/6 tbsp butter

1 egg, beaten

575ml/1 pint/2½ cups creamy milk

Let the raisins steep in the rum for 20 minutes. Grease a gratin dish or other shallow baking dish and pre-heat the oven to 150°C (300°F). Mix the baking powder into the flour then rub in the butter. Beat the egg and milk into the flour mixture until it is smooth. Finally, stir in the raisins and rum and pour into the dish. Bake for 30–40 minutes or until a knife-tip slid into the centre comes out clean. Serve warm or cold.

Seed-Cake

The ladies of *Cranford* ate seed-cake, and it was generous slices of Miss Temple's seed-cake that delighted the half-starved Jane and Helen Burns in *Jane Eyre*. It used to be a staple in both bakery shops and home kitchens, and was rivalled only by muffins on the tea tables of Nineteenth-Century novels. It seems to be out of fashion now, but is nonetheless delicious.

4 eggs, separated

225g/8oz/1 cup butter at room temperature

225g/8oz/1 cup sugar

225g/8oz/2 cups plain flour

1½ tsp baking powder

1 tsp powdered coriander

85g/3oz/½ cup candied orange peel

3½ tsp (or more to taste) caraway seeds

Line a deep 18cm (7-inch) cake tin or a springform tin with baking parchment. Pre-heat the oven to 180°C (350°F). Whisk the egg whites until they form soft peaks and put in the fridge. Cream the butter and sugar until pale and fluffy. Combine the flour with the baking powder and coriander. Mix a couple of tablespoons of this plus one yolk into the butter mixture. Repeat this with the remaining yolks, then mix in the remaining flour. Stir in the candied peel and 3 teaspoons of the caraway seeds. Finally fold in the beaten egg whites and gently turn the mixture into the cake tin. Scatter the last half-teaspoon of the caraway seeds on top. Bake for 55–65 minutes or until a skewer poked into the middle comes out clean. Cool in the tin on a wire rack for 15–20 minutes, then remove. Cool then store in an airtight container.

Sponge Cake

For at least three centuries various kinds of sponge cakes have been a favourite companion to a cup of tea. Jane Austen confessed she was 'always interested in the purchase of a sponge cake', and Mrs. Gaskell's Cranford ladies made them for their tea parties.

70g/2½oz/5 tablespoons unsalted butter

1 tbsp water

¼ tsp vanilla essence, optional

140g/5oz/1¼ cups plain flour

½ tsp baking powder

4 eggs

225g/8oz/1 cup caster sugar

1 tbsp icing sugar

Pre-heat the oven to 190°C (375°F). Line the base of a 23cm (9-inch) sandwich cake tin with parchment and butter and flour the edges. Melt the butter with the water without letting it bubble. Add the vanilla and set it aside to cool but don't let it firm up. Combine the flour and baking powder. In a large bowl, whisk the eggs and sugar until they are pale, foamy and about 5 times swollen in bulk. The beater – ideally an electric one – should leave trails in the mixture.

Stir in the melted butter, then gently fold in a third of the flour. When mixed, fold in another third and finally fold in the rest. Pour into the tin and bake for 22–25 minutes or until golden and a toothpick or skewer poked in the middle comes out clean. Let cool in the tin on a rack. When cool run a knife around the edge to loosen the cake and turn out. What was formerly the top will now be the bottom. At this point you can simply dust with icing sugar. Or slice in half and fill with jam and buttercream or whipped cream and strawberries or raspberries. If you make this in two 6-inch tins, you will have two layers, so no need to slice. Baking time will be slightly shorter.

CHOCOLATE CAKE

In *The Last September* Elizabeth Bowen refers to a family whose speciality was 'a chocolate cake made by a charm'. You need no magic spell to make this chocolate cake because it's so easy – and so chocolatey. With just a simple snow-flurry of icing sugar, its very plainness makes it good with tea.

140g/5oz/1¼ cups plain flour

55g/2oz/½ cup cocoa powder

1 tsp bicarbonate of soda

100g/3½oz 70 per cent bittersweet chocolate

225g/8oz/1 cup soft unsalted butter

280g/10oz/1½ cups muscovado sugar

1 tsp vanilla essence

2 eggs

175ml/6fl oz/¾ cup very hot water

1 tbsp icing sugar

Pre-heat the oven to 180°C (350°F). Grease the edge of a 23cm (9-inch) springform tin and line the base with parchment. Mix the flour, cocoa and bicarbonate of soda and set aside. Melt the chocolate, either in a microwave or in a small bowl set over a pan of simmering water. Let it cool but not harden. In a large bowl, beat the butter and muscovado sugar until light. Add the vanilla essence and beat in the eggs one at a time, and then the chocolate. Mix in about a third of the flour, followed by a third of the water. Repeat this step until you have used all the flour and all or most of the water, and the mixture is a little sloppier than most cakes. Turn it into the prepared tin and bake for 25–30 minutes or until a skewer poked in the middle comes out clean. Cool on a wire rack for about 30 minutes, then run a knife between the cake and the tin and release the clasp. Cool until cold. Sieve icing sugar on the top before serving.

ORANGE CAKE WITH CHOCOLATE-ORANGE ICING

In Elizabeth Bowen's *The Last September* Mrs. Vermont gorges on orange cake. Orange cakes are also favourites in Molly Keane's Irish novels.

Cake:

3 eggs

115g/4oz/1 stick butter

115g/4oz/½ cup sugar

175g/6oz/1½ cups flour

1 tsp baking powder

¼ tsp powdered cinnamon

zest of one large orange

juice of half the orange

Icing:

225g/8oz/1½ cups sifted icing sugar

juice of half an orange

1 tbsp shredless orange marmalade

about 20 Cadbury's orange-flavoured Snaps or about 55g (2oz) orange-flavoured chocolate

Line a deep 18cm (7-inch) cake tin with paper and pre-heat the oven to 180°C (350°F). Separate the eggs and whisk the whites until they form soft (not stiff) peaks. Keep in the fridge while you cream the butter and sugar together. Mix the flour with the baking powder and cinnamon. Add a tablespoon of this mixture to the sugar and butter along with one egg yolk, and mix well. Repeat this step twice more, adding the orange zest with the final egg yolk. Now add the rest of the flour mixture along with about a tablespoon of the orange juice. You want a soft consistency; if the mixture is stiff, add more of the orange juice. Finally, fold in the egg whites, and then gently spoon into the prepared tin. Bake for 30–40 minutes or until a skewer poked in the middle comes out clean. Let cool in the tin for about 15 minutes, then remove and finish cooling on a wire rack. Chill before icing. To make the icing, sift the icing sugar into a bowl and make a well in the centre. Add about a tablespoon of orange juice and stir until smooth. Add more orange juice only if needed to make the icing spreadable. Heat the marmalade in a small pan with a teaspoon of water. Brush it over the chilled cake. Now spread on the icing. If using Snaps, arrange about half around the edge while the icing is still soft, and break the rest into shards to scatter over the centre and the sides. Alternatively, grate the orange-flavoured chocolate and toss it over the cake.

WALNUT CAKE

Fuller's tea rooms served slices of a deliciously moist walnut cake. Customers could also purchase the cake to take home, and many people have fond memories of having it for special teas. Among them is Charles Ryder of Evelyn Waugh's *Brideshead Revisited*, who serves it to his pompous cousin, Jasper.

Cake:

225g/8oz/2 sticks butter

225g/8oz/1 cup sugar

3 eggs

225g/8oz/2 cups plain flour

½ tsp mace

1 tsp baking powder

115g/4oz walnuts, coarsely ground

Icing:

1 egg white

175g/6oz icing sugar

8–10 walnut halves

Pre-heat the oven to 160°C (325°F) degrees and grease a 20cm (8-inch) springform tin. Line the base with parchment paper and dust the sides lightly with flour. Cream the butter and sugar until pale and fluffy. Add the eggs one at a time, beating after each addition and adding a tablespoon of the flour with the last one. Combine the flour, mace and baking powder and mix into the butter mixture. Fold in the ground walnuts. Bake in the centre of the oven for 45–55 minutes or until a skewer poked in the centre comes out clean. Cool on a wire rack for half an hour, then release the spring on the pan and continue cooling. Chill in the fridge for an hour before icing, then turn the cake upside down so what was the bottom during cooking now presents a flat top. Whisk the egg white until it stands in soft peaks. Add half the icing sugar and whisk again, then add the remaining icing sugar and whisk until bulky and the whisk leaves traces in the mixture. To ice the cake spread icing around the sides and gradually work it upwards and over the top. Arrange the walnut halves around the edge.

Sandwiches and Savoury Dishes

CUCUMBER SANDWICHES

Cucumber sandwiches taste so deliciously more than the sum of their parts that it's understandable that Algy eats the whole plateful while waiting for Lady Bracknell's arrival in the opening scene of Oscar Wilde's *The Importance of Being Earnest*.

½ cucumber, peeled and thinly sliced

salt

12 thin slices buttered white bread, crusts removed

white pepper

Put the thin slices of cucumber on a plate and sprinkle with salt. Leave for 20 minutes then rinse to get rid of excess salt and pat with paper towels to dry. Arrange even layers of sliced cucumber on 6 bread slices; dust lightly with white pepper and top with the other bread slices. Cut the sandwiches into triangles or fingers.

LOBSTER AND LETTUCE SANDWICHES

With these sandwiches Birdie gets the attention of the man she fancies in Molly Keane's *Loving Without Tears*. 'A wonderful cuisine,' he murmured as he watched her making them.

1 lobster (about 550g/1¼ pounds), boiled

salt and white pepper to taste

1 tbsp chopped parsley

1 tsp snipped chives (or more to taste)

2 tbsp Greek yogurt or mayonnaise

few drops lemon juice to taste

1 lettuce heart

Remove the meat from the tail and the claws of the lobster. Also mine the legs. Set aside any coral you find. Cut the lobster into small but not fragmentary pieces. Lightly salt and pepper it to taste, scatter the parsley and chives over it, and stir in the Greek yoghurt using just enough to bind the lobster. Taste and add lemon juice or more salt and pepper as you see fit. Tear the lettuce into pieces. Sandwich the lobster and lettuce in buttered granary bread, sprinkling in any coral as you go. Cut the sandwiches in half, but don't make them too weeny.

SMOKED SALMON AND LEMON MASCARPONE SANDWICHES

Salmon-farming has cut the price of smoked salmon so it is no longer the super-expensive luxury it was just a few years ago, and smoked salmon sandwiches are now staples on Afternoon Tea menus.

115g/4oz mascarpone

1 tbsp milk

1 tbsp finely grated lemon zest plus few drops of juice

4–6 slices wholemeal or granary bread or brioche

85g/3oz smoked salmon

mustard and cress or chopped parsley for garnish

Blend the mascarpone with the milk, then stir in the lemon zest. Spread this on slices of bread or brioche. Top with the smoked salmon, squeezing a few drops of lemon juice on it. Cover with the remaining mascarpone-covered slices of bread. Remove the crusts and cut into triangles or fingers. Scatter the mustard and cress or parsley sparingly on top.

HAZELNUT SANDWICHES

All the animals contribute something in Alison Uttley's *Little Grey Rabbit's Party*. Squirrel 'found hoards of nuts which she ground in a bowl' to make the hazelnut sandwiches for the party.

225g/8oz hazelnuts without skins

115g/4oz cream cheese

1 tbsp honey

petals from 6–8 marigolds (calendula), optional

fruit bread or malt loaf

Toast the hazelnuts for about 6–8 minutes in a 180°C (350°F) oven or for about 2 minutes in a microwave. They are ready when they are caramel-colour and deliciously fragrant. Whizz them in a food processor or a blender until the texture is like rough crumbs. Cool then mix with the cream cheese and honey and about half the petals if you are using them. Make sandwiches with raisiny fruit bread or malt loaf with crusts removed. Scatter some of the remaining petals: some on top of the filling, leaving some to garnish the sandwich plate. (This filling is also good made with pecans.)

TURKEY AND BACON PASTE

In pre-fridge days potted meat and fish was made by mixing leftovers with butter, packing the mixture in a crock then covering with a layer of clarified butter, which sealed out the air and preserved it. Nineteenth-Century canning technology turned potted foods into cheap pastes, which became popular sandwich fillings. Diva offered potted meat sandwiches in her tea room in *Trouble for Lucia* by E.F. Benson, and in Molly Keane's *Good Behaviour* greedy Aroon St Charles finds the Crowhurst twins' 'fish paté sandwiches irresistible'. Food processors take the work out of such recipes. They are as thrifty as ever, and taste streets better than commercial pastes. Chicken, rabbit or pork could replace the turkey in this recipe, and ham could fill in for bacon. Vary the proportions of meat depending on what you have, and taste as you go to judge how much seasoning you like.

85g/3oz/3 slices back bacon

85g/3oz leftover cooked turkey

115g/4oz/1 stick butter at room temperature

about 1 tsp dried sage or thyme

¼ tsp mace or nutmeg

1 tsp Worcestershire sauce

white pepper to taste

Cook the bacon for 3–4 minutes or until done but not crisp. Put the bacon and turkey in a food processor and pulse until they are chopped. Now add half the butter, the sage or thyme, mace or nutmeg and the Worcestershire sauce. Whizz until mixed, then add the rest of the butter and process until smooth. Now taste. Add pepper plus more drops of Worcestershire sauce or extra thyme to suit your palate. For use within 5 days, simply put into a dish, press cling film over the surface and keep in the fridge. For keeping up to 3 weeks pour a quarter-inch layer of melted butter on top and keep in the fridge. Serve in sandwiches, adding capers or chutney to taste.

SALMON AND PRAWN PASTE

Aroon St Charles longed to know the recipe for the 'wonderful potted fish' the Crowhurst twins make in Molly Keane's *Good Behaviour*. Here's an easy recipe for a fish paté.

175g/6oz/¾ cup flaked poached salmon

115g/4oz/1 stick unsalted butter at room temperature

about ½ tsp Worcestershire sauce

sea salt to taste

cayenne pepper to taste

about ⅛–¼ tsp freshly grated nutmeg

85g/3oz cooked peeled prawns plus extra for garnish

Put the flaked salmon and the butter in a food processor and whiz to combine. Add the ½ teaspoon Worcestershire sauce, salt, a dash of cayenne, and ¼ teaspoon nutmeg. Process again and taste. Adjust the Worcestershire sauce, salt, pepper and nutmeg as you see fit. Finally, add the prawns and pulse so they stay a bit chunky. Pour into a greased dish and cover with cling film. Chill before using in sandwiches.

SARDINE AND TOMATO PASTE

Early Twentieth-Century descriptions of tea parties invariably mention sardines. For high tea they were served with tomatoes as at the Suttons' in Arnold Bennett's *Anna of the Five Towns*. For afternoon tea they were mashed or made into a paste for sandwiches. This paste is easy and tastier than those you buy in the supermarket.

106g/3¾oz tin sardines in olive oil

40g/1½oz/3 tbsp butter at room temperature

1 tsp tomato paste

1 tsp Worcestershire sauce

cayenne pepper, salt, black pepper and lemon juice to taste

Without being too obsessive about it, drain the olive oil from the sardines. Mash them with the butter, then mash in the tomato paste, about half the Worcestershire sauce, a dash of cayenne, salt and a grind or two of black pepper. Mash until smooth, then taste. Using tiny amounts at a time, add the remaining Worcestershire sauce, and more tomato paste, cayenne, salt, pepper and drops of lemon juice until it tastes the way you like. Pack into a ramekin or other small pot and cover with cling film. Refrigerate and serve within 2–3 days.

Savoury Dishes

VEAL AND HAM PIE

In Beatrix Potter's *The Pie and the Patty-Pan* the cat Ribby makes a mouse and bacon pie, while the dog Duchess makes a veal and ham pie. Though she says she can't bear to eat mouse, Duchess gobbles Ribby's pie believing it's her own veal and ham pie. Presumably, then, mouse and bacon tastes the same as veal and ham! Beatrix Potter lived in the Lake District, where meat pies often include potato for moistness. Meat pies are typical high tea fare in the North.

Filling:

500g/1lb stewing veal

250g/9oz slice of ham

5 tbsp chopped fresh parsley

grated zest of 1 lemon

1 tbsp plain flour

2–3 large potatoes, peeled

white pepper to taste

Pastry:

225g/8oz/1 cup flour

½ tsp baking powder

115g/4oz/½ cup lard

chilled water

1 tbsp cream

Grease a deep pie dish. Pre-heat the oven to 180°C (350°F). Chop the veal and ham into little bits, but don't mince. With your hands, mix the meats with the parsley and lemon zest. Finally toss with the flour. Slice the potatoes thinly (about ¼ inch) and make a thin layer of them covering the bottom of the dish. Season with pepper. Cover with the meat mixture, and then another thin layer of peppered potato slices. Cover the dish with foil and bake for an hour or until the potatoes are tender. Increase the oven to 200°C (400°F). Make the pastry by mixing the flour and baking powder, and rubbing the lard into it. Add just enough chilled water to make a dough, and roll it out to cover the pie. Brush the top with cream, and cut some slashes for steam to escape. Return to the oven and bake for 20 minutes or until the pastry is golden. Good hot (as Duchess ate it) or cold.

PAKORAS

Indians like something savoury as well as something sweet with tea. In Kirin Desai's *Inheritance of Loss* the terrorists who invade the judge's house demand pakoras, a favourite vegetable fritter.

Vegetables:

1 medium aubergine

1 large potato, boiled for 10 minutes

2 small sweet peppers, red or green

12 cauliflower florets

Batter:

225g/8oz/2 cups chickpea flour (besan)

½ tsp salt

¼ tsp cayenne

1 tsp baking powder

about 600ml/20 fl oz/2½ cups vegetable oil

Slice the aubergine into 5mm (¼-inch) pieces and sprinkle with salt. Leave for 30 minutes then rinse and dry. Slice the potato 5mm (¼-inch) thick. Cut the peppers into 10mm (½-inch) strips. The cauliflower florets should be about 15mm (¾-inch) thick. Make the batter by mixing the chickpea flour with the salt, cayenne and baking powder.

Slowly stir in 250ml (9 fl oz, 1 cup) cold water until smooth. Add more water if needed to make it the thickness of Yorkshire pudding batter. Heat the oil in a wok or wide pan. When a drop of batter quickly rises to the surface and sizzles, dip 8–10 vegetable pieces in the batter and cook them 4–5 minutes per side or until golden. Add more as they get done, but don't crowd the pan. Drain on kitchen paper and keep the pakoras warm until all are cooked. Serve with chutney. Sweet potato, courgettes and butternut squash can also be cooked in this way.

Tea Eggs

Boiled eggs often appear in English teas; so do egg sandwiches. In China, tiny tea-cooked quail eggs may be served with tea. Hen and duck eggs are also popular – with beer too.

10 hen or duck eggs or 20 quail eggs

1¼ litres/40 fl oz/2 pints/5 cups water

15g/½oz/2 tbsp black tea

2 whole star anise

6cm/2½-inch stick cinnamon

8 black peppercorns

1½ tsp salt

Put the eggs and water into a large saucepan; bring to the boil and simmer for 8–10 minutes for hen or duck eggs, 5 minutes for quail eggs. Remove the eggs to a bowl of chilled water. Add the tea, star anise, cinnamon, peppercorns and salt to the pan. Take the eggs, and tap them all over with the back of a spoon so the shell cracks. Leave the cracked shell on the eggs and return to the pan. Bring back to simmering again. Simmer for 45 minutes then remove from the heat. Let the eggs cool in the liquid. Keep in the fridge, still in the shell, until you want to use them (they are fine for 5–6 days). Shell them for serving at high tea, and halve or quarter hen or duck eggs. Alternatively, chop and mix with just enough softened butter to make a sandwich filling. Watercress teams well with tea eggs – or indeed, ordinary hard-boiled eggs.

WELSH RAREBIT

Few dishes are simpler than Welsh rarebit, and few have a more mysterious name. Why rarebit? Welsh rabbit is an alternative form, (though rarebit is generally used in Wales), but why should something as common as cheese be called rare or a rabbit? Authorities have no answers, but Thackeray, Sir Walter Scott and Fanny Burney all enjoyed Welsh rarebit. D.H. Lawrence's *Kangaroo* notes the importance of cayenne: 'What an excellent Welsh rarebit,' he said. 'If there were a little red pepper.' 'Red pepper?' cried Victoria. 'There is!' Recipes vary widely; some have only cheese – typically Caerphilly, Cheddar or Cheshire – but others, including this one, use milk or eggs to create a more lush mixture. Welsh rarebit is high tea fare, and a staple on tea-room menus in Wales.

¼ tsp mustard powder

55g/2oz sliced or grated cheese

1 tbsp milk

2 egg yolks, beaten

cayenne or white pepper to taste

2 slices hot buttered toast

Turn on the grill. Mix the mustard to a thin paste with a teaspoon of water and set aside. In a small pan melt the cheese with the milk over low heat. As soon as it melts stir in the mustard and the beaten egg yolks. Stir over low heat until everything has amalgamated and thickened, then season to your taste with cayenne or white pepper. Spread it on the buttered toast. Put on a baking sheet or heat-proof plate and slide under the grill for a minute or two or until patched with brown. Eat immediately.

Glossary of Food Terms

British	American
Almond essence	Almond extract
Aubergine	Eggplant
Bicarbonate of soda	Baking soda
Candied peel	Crystallized peel
Caster sugar	Superfine sugar
Cling film	Plastic wrap
Cornflour	Cornstarch
Dessicated coconut	Shredded coconut
Double cream	Heavy cream
Glacé cherries	Crystallized cherries
Golden syrup	A cane syrup, available in some US stores (do not substitute corn or maple syrup)
Granary bread	Seeded wholewheat bread
Icing sugar	Confectioner's sugar
Muscovado sugar	Light brown sugar
Mustard and cress	Mustard, cress or other small sprouts
Plain flour	All-purpose flour
Prawns	Large shrimp (41–60 size)
Sandwich cake tin	Layer cake pan
Strong flour	Bread flour
Sultanas	Golden raisins
Treacle	Molasses
Vanilla essence	Vanilla extract

Select List of Tea Rooms

BRITAIN has thousands of tea rooms and tea shops, and so many are so good that a complete list of these national treasures is not possible in a small space. The following tea rooms all offer delicious food, stimulating pots of tea, and in most cases, a charming or interesting setting.

Acorn Whole Food Restaurant and Coffee House
26 Sandford Avenue,
Church Stretton,
Shropshire
SY6 6BW
Tel: 01694 722495

This charmingly located vegetarian restaurant offers twenty kinds of tea and stupendous slices of homey cakes using organic ingredients.

Attic
115 Coldharbour Road,
Redland,
Bristol
BS6 7SD
Tel: 0117 909 0357
www.attictea.co.uk

Specialising in Chinese tea, Attic gives tea-lovers the chance to try myriad teas – including a green tea latte – served in glass pots that show the leaves elegantly unfurling. Food selections are designed to complement the many speciality teas.

Betty's Café Tea Rooms
1 Parliament Street,
Harrogate,
Yorkshire
HG1 2QU
Tel: 01423 877300
www.bettys.co.uk

Betty's is a beloved Yorkshire institution, famous for Fat Rascals – an especially plump scone – which vie with Yorkshire tea bread, parkin, sloe-gin fruitcake and an array of European-style pastries. Betty's serves afternoon tea with either its own Taylor's Yorkshire tea or one of the many teas sold in the shop. China Rose Petal is especially delicious. Betty's has branches in York, Northallerton, Ilkley, and at the RHS Garden at Harlow Carr in Harrogate.

The Cadogan Hotel
75 Sloane Street,
Knightsbridge,
London
SW1X 9SG
Tel: 0207 201 6614
www.Cadogan.com

Lily Langtry lived at the Cadogan; Edward VII kept rooms there and Oscar Wilde often stayed in Room 118. Locals love the place, and many come for afternoon tea with its array of sandwiches, pretty pastries and warm-from-the-oven scones. This makes reservations a good idea.

The Coffee Shop at Edwards China
2–10 Market Lane,
Hanley,
Stoke-on-Trent
ST1 1LA
Tel: 01782 260345
www.edwardschina.co.uk

Set in Arnold Bennett's home town in the very heart of the Potteries, Edwards combines a china shop with a tea room that serves hot Staffordshire oatcakes with various fillings. Their superlative scones were voted the best in Staffordshire.

De Grey's
5–6 Broad Street,
Ludlow,
Shropshire
SY8 1NG
Tel: 01584 872764
www.degreys.co.uk

Beautifully set in a black-and-white-timbered Elizabethan building beneath Ludlow's Buttercross, De Grey's offers tea with breads and pastries from its own bakeries.

De Wynn's Tea and Coffee House
55 Church Street,
Falmouth,
Cornwall
TR11 3DS
Tel: 01326 319259
www.dewynns.co.uk

De Wynn's decoration preserves the style and spirit of its Grade II listed Eighteenth-Century building, while its menu emphasises the luscious cream, pleasing cheeses, and local berries of Cornwall. Among their teas is Tregothnan from England's only tea garden, located nearby on the bank of the River Fal.

The Dorchester
Park Lane,
London
W1A 2H1
Tel: 020 7317 6499
www.dorchesterhotel.com

Choose from over thirty loose teas, and sip it sitting on the softest of sofas with a daily-changing menu of sandwiches, cakes and scones. Excellence and opulence are the hallmarks here.

Fortnum and Mason's
181 Piccadilly,
London
WIA 1ER
Tel: 020 7734 8040
www.fortnumandmason.com

Fortnum's sells a huge variety of teas from around the world including from Tregothnan in Cornwall, Britain's only tea plantation. Afternoon tea in the St James Restaurant has sandwiches, scones and cakes; high tea offers such substantial dishes as Welsh Rarebit with Back Bacon or Mushrooms on Toasted Brioche – a good pre-theatre meal.

Greystone House Tea Room
Stainton,
Penrith,
Cumbria
CA11 0EF
Tel: 01768 866952
www.greystonehousefarm.co.uk

Just off Junction 40 of the M6 near Penrith, this farm-based tea room uses local organic foods in their tea and lunch dishes.

Grosvenor Hotel
Eastgate Street,
Chester
CH1 1LT
Tel: 01244 324024
www.chestergrosvenor.com

Enjoy tea in the Library as the hotel's perfectly trained staff seat you on its deep-cushioned couches and chairs. Afternoon tea includes a selection of finger sandwiches from the Michelin-starred kitchen plus scones, clotted cream and mouthwatering patisserie. Champagne, of course, if you'd like it.

Gwalia Tea Room
The Museum of Welsh Life,
St Fagans,
Cardiff
CF5 6XB
Tel: 029 2056 6985
www.museumwales.ac.uk

This 1920s tea room is above the Gwalia Stores, which were moved from Bridgend to the museum. It offers homemade cakes and Welsh specialities including an excellent Welsh rarebit of Y Fenni cheese.

Harrods
The Georgian Restaurant,
Brompton Road,
London
SW1X 7XL
Tel: 020 7225 6800
www.Harrods.com

The Georgian Restaurant was opened to celebrate the coronation of King George V, and it's still an elegant venue for tea. Connoisseurs can ask for their favourite tea, or choose from the many listed on the menu.

Hazelmere Café and Bakery
1 Yewbarrow Terrace,
Grange-over-Sands,
Cumbria
LA11 6ED
Tel: 01539 532972
www.hazelmerecafe.co.uk

Choose from over thirty teas from India, Sri Lanka, China and Africa and enjoy it with baked goods, including Cumberland Rum Nicky, made in its own bakery. This friendly tea room won the Tea Guild's Tea Room of the Year award in 2006.

Hive on the Quay
Cadwgan Place,
Aberaeron,
West Wales
SA46 OBU
Tel: 01545 570445
www.hiveonthequay.co.uk

Overlooking a colourful row of Georgian houses, Hive on the Quay features sandwiches of local crab and their famous honey ice cream, plus teas with scones, rosemary biscuits and excellent bara brith. A nearby board records Dylan Thomas's life in Aberaeron in the 1940s.

Jones Café
93 Queen's Road,
Leicester
LE2 1TT
Tel: 0116 270 8830

Located in a lively student area of Leicester, this popular spot serves only home-made food with imaginative offerings, many of them vegetarian, and lots of varieties of tea to choose from.

Juri's The Old Bakery Tea Shoppe
High Street,
Winchcombe,
Cheltenham,
Gloucestershire
CL54 5LJ
Tel: 01242 602469
www.Juris-Tearoom.co.uk

Juri is the Cordon Bleu-trained chef who prepares the savoury dishes, sandwiches and enticing cakes served in the pretty conservatory and gardens of this Cotswold tea room. The selection of teas is wide, with many Japanese teas reflecting the owners' Japanese heritage.

Katie's Tea Rooms
38 Watergate Street,
Chester
CH1 2LA
Tel: 01244 400322

Katie's is in a Grade II listed merchant's house built in 1325 on the famous Rows of Chester. Wattle and daub construction is still visible as are the arches, beams and fireplaces from later eras. Good selection of teas with toasted tea cakes, crumpets and other tea-time fare.

Kind Kyttock's Kitchen
Cross Wynd,
Falkland,
Cupar,
Fife
KY15 7BE
Tel: 01337 857477

In days of yore Kind Kyttock earned her name by feeding tired travellers. This tea room is similarly renowned for the joys it provides: fires in winter, a good selection of teas, and homey Scottish specialities such as scones, drop scones, and shortbread.

Low Sizergh Barn Tea Rooms
Low Sizergh Farm,
Sizergh,
Kendal,
Cumbria – the Lake District
LA8 8AE
Tel: 01539 560426
www.lowsizerghbarn.co.uk

Watch the milking of cows that provide milk for your tea and cream for your scones from an Elizabethan barn, now cleverly converted into a tea room with a huge window overlooking the milking parlour. Much of the food is from local organic farms.

The Mock Turtle
4 Pool Valley,
Brighton,
East Sussex
BN1 1NJ
Tel: 01273 327380

It's worth visiting Brighton just to enjoy the delicious meringues which are available in three mouth-watering flavours at this attractive tea room, close to Brighton Pier and the Pavilion. Cakes are baked on the premises, including the enormous freshly made doughnuts. A breakfast favourite amongst locals, as well as the perfect venue for afternoon tea.

Ollerton Watermill Tea Shop
Market Place,
Ollerton,
Newark,
Nottinghamshire
NG22 9AA
Tel: 01623 822549

At this 1713 watermill set in Robin Hood Country visitors can watch the wheel still turning, ogle the ducks on the pond, and enjoy the teas, cakes and scones at a tea room that regularly wins the Tea Guild's accolades.

Osborne House
17 North Parade,
Llandudno,
Conwy
LL30 2LP
Tel: 01492 860330
www.osbornehouse.com

Marine paintings, marble tables, sparkling chandeliers and yellow sofas create a lovely tea-time setting. Watch the waves roll into the bay or nestle into a couch and admire the décor while enjoying excellent bara brith or scones with your tea.

Quayside Tea Rooms
Lawrenny Quay,
Lawrenny,
Pembrokeshire
SA68 0PR
Tel: 01646 888479

Sail boats bob in the Daugleddau estuary in the Pembrokeshire National Park while you enjoy tea with the Quayside's crab sandwiches and cakes that include the popular Lemon Thing, banoffi tart, raspberry cheesecake and various chocolate cakes.

Peacock's
65 Waterside,
Ely,
Cambridgeshire
CB7 4AU
Tel: 01353 661100

Choose from over fifty types of tea served with home-cooked foods in this friendly tea room packed with tea memorabilia and tea books. Choose Afternoon Tea or their special Pink Perfection Tea: smoked salmon sandwiches served with a glass of sparkling rosé, scones with cream and jam, and rose-petal tea. Peacock's won the Tea Guild's 2007 Award for Top Tea Place.

The Pump Room
Stall Street,
Bath,
Avon
BA1 1LZ
Tel: 01225 444477
www.searcys.co.uk

Jane Austen's characters came to Bath to take the waters, and you can still do that at the fountain in The Pump Room. But tea served under the elegant chandelier tastes better. Food choices include sandwiches, scones, pastries, plus dishes based on cheeses of the south-west.

Roses Tea Rooms
23 Milner Road,
Heswall,
Wirral
CH60 5RT
Tel: 0151 342 9912
www.rosestearooms.co.uk

The child-friendliness of Roses is reflected in healthful locally-sourced ingredients, a nursery tea menu with cinnamon toast, and a welcome for nursing mothers. But everyone else also has a lovely time eating hearty sandwiches and handsome slices of the excellent home-made cakes. Lavender and rose scones are a speciality.

Sally Lunn's
4 North Parade Passage,
Bath,
Avon
BA1 1NX
Tel: 01225 461634
www.sallylunns.co.uk

Sally Lunn supposedly came to Bath in the Seventeenth Century and made good by selling a breakfast bread that now bears her name. Her house is a major tourist attraction and an excellent spot for a Sally Lunn tea with either cream and jam or a savoury topping.

Savoy Hotel
The Strand,
London
WC2 0EU
Tel: 0207 836 4343
www.fairmont.com

Arnold Bennett based his novel *Imperial Palace* on his many stays at the Savoy. Oscar Wilde was arrested there. George Gershwin gave the European premiere of *Rhapsody in Blue*. Another pianist now entertains afternoon tea guests in the Thames Foyer. People come to celebrate, so champagne often accompanies the traditional tea-time sandwiches, scones, and pastries.

Sharrow Bay Country House Hotel
Ullswater,
Penrith,
Cumbria
CA10 2LZ
Tel: 01768 486301
www.sharrow-bay.com

Lake District residents often celebrate birthdays and engagements with afternoon tea at Sharrow Bay – and they make sure to bring their appetites. Served on Royal Worcester china, tea includes finger sandwiches, a three-tiered cake stand freighted with home-baked scones, short-bread and tea bread, followed by toasted tea cakes and a selection of yet more cakes, including chocolate gateaux and Swiss roll. Eating it all is impossible, so anything left is packed to take home. With all this you get sublime views of the lake and gardens.

Shipp's Tearooms
4 Park Street,
London
SE1 9AB
Tel: 020 7407 2692
www.shippstearooms.co.uk

Across from Borough Market, Shipp's has embroidered cloth-covered tables, sweet posies, and charming china. Victoria sponge, chocolate sandwich, lemon drizzle and carrot cake all wave their little hands, begging to be chosen. There's a fine selection of teas to enjoy as you rest from the market bustle or watch the passing throng.

Sir George Newnes Tearoom
14 Lee Road,
Lynton,
Devon
EX35 6HW
Tel: 01598 753478

This pretty tea room in the Exmoor National Park offers both a Ginger Tea and a Pixie Tea – for those who want just one scone.

St Tudno Hotel and Restaurant
North Parade, Promenade
Llandudno,
North Wales
LL30 2LP
Tel: 01492 874411
www.st-tudno.co.uk

Little Alice Liddell, for whom Lewis Caroll wrote *Alice in Wonderland* stayed here on family holidays. Famous for its food, St Tudno's serves tea in its Victorian sitting room, where it's easy to imagine the Liddells enjoying tea before the fireplace. A wide selection of teas and Welsh specialities are on offer at St Tudno's today.

The Willow Tea Rooms
217 Sauchiehall Street,
Glasgow
G2 3EX
Tel: 0141 332 0521
www.willowtearooms.co.uk

Aesthetically no tea room in Britain is more famous than the Willow Tea Rooms designed entirely by Charles Rennie Mackintosh. The original tea room has been lovingly refurbished into a beautiful setting for a large and appetising tea menu that includes many Scottish specialities.

Y Gegin Fawr
Aberdaron,
Pwllheli,
Gwynedd
LL53 8BE
Tel: 01758 760359
www.ygeginfawr.co.uk

Y Gegin Fawr means The Big Kitchen. Actually the tiny Thirteenth-Century building was the community house for pilgrims waiting to sail to Bardsey, the fabled off-shore island of 20,000 saints. Tea is served in the low-ceilinged dormitory where they slept. This unpretentious tea room serves good cakes and a decent Welsh rarebit.

Yew Tree Farm Tea Room
Yew Tree Farm,
Coniston,
Cumbria
LA21 8DP
Tel: 01539 441433
www.yewtree-farm.co.uk

In the dire economic days of the 1930s Beatrix Potter lent furniture and crockery to her tenants at Yew Tree Farm so they could open a tea room in the parlour. You can still enjoy tea at her tables, or sit in the pretty garden and gaze at the farmhouse – the location for the Renée Zellweger film *Miss Potter*. Local products are featured, including the farm's Herdwick lamb – a northern breed that Potter strove to preserve.

Select Bibliography

Bramah, Edward, *Tea and Coffee Walk Around London*. Christan LeComte Publishing, 2005.

Chalker, Brian, *Cook-ups of World War Two*. Bristol: Redcliffe Press Ltd., 1987.

Collingham, Lizzie, *Curry: A Tale of Cooks and Conquerors*. Oxford: Oxford University Press, 2006.

Davies, Jennifer, *The Wartime Kitchen and Garden: The Home Front 1939–45*. London: BBC Books, 1993.

Emmerson, Robin, *British Teapots and Tea Drinking 1700–1850*. London: Her Majesty's Stationery Office, 1992.

Heiss, Mary Lou and Robert J., *The Story of Tea: A Cultural History and Drinking Guide*. Berkeley: Ten Speed Press, 2007.

Macfarlane, Alan and Iris, *Green Gold: The Empire of Tea*. London: Ebury, 2003.

Mason, Laura with Brown, Catherine, *Traditional Foods of Britain: An Inventory*. Prospect Books, 1999.

Mintz, Stanley, *Sweetness and Power*. New York: The Viking Press, 1985.

Okakura, Kakuzo, *The Book of Tea*. Boston: Tuttle Publishing, 2000.

Pettigrew, Jane, *Tea and Infusions: A Connoisseur's Guide*. Carlton Books, 1999.

Schivelbusch, Wolfgang, *Tastes of Paradise*. New York: Pantheon Books, 1992.

Shalleck, Jamie, *Tea*. New York: The Viking Press, 1972.

Spencer, Colin, *British Food: An Extraordinary Thousand Years of History*. London: Grub Street, 2002.

Select Bibliography

Ukers, William H., *The Romance of Tea: An Outline History of Tea and Tea-Drinking Through Sixteen Hundred Years*. New York: Alfred A. Knopf, 1936.

Index

Index

Index